Anonymous

Biblical Anthology

A Collection of Passages Illustrating the Purity and Morality of the Holy

Bible

Anonymous

Biblical Anthology
A Collection of Passages Illustrating the Purity and Morality of the Holy Bible

ISBN/EAN: 9783337098254

Printed in Europe, USA, Canada, Australia, Japan

Cover: Foto ©Lupo / pixelio.de

More available books at **www.hansebooks.com**

BIBLICAL ANTHOLOGY

A COLLECTION OF PASSAGES

ILLUSTRATING THE

PURITY AND MORALITY

OF THE

HOLY BIBLE.

All scripture is given by inspiration of God, and is profitable for doctrine, for reproof, for correction, for instruction in righteousness.— 2 Timothy, iii, 16.

TORONTO: ONT.
JONES & BELFORD.
1881.

PREFACE.

The recent nefarious attempt, by certain evil-disposed persons not having the fear of God before their eyes, to assoil the purity and corrupt the morality of the people of Ontario, by the importation of Paine's "Age of Reason" and Voltaire's "Pocket Theology," is unfortunately a matter of too great notoriety. The confiscation of the works by the Collector of Customs at Toronto, on the ground of obscenity and immorality, will, it is to be feared, have the effect of greatly promoting their circulation and sale. It has therefore been thought desirable to issue a small volume which should act both as a prophylactic against, and an antidote to, the poisonous influence which the works named are calculated to exert. The Holy Scriptures are of course the source whence the desired panacea may be best obtained. The shape which the present volume takes,—that of a collection of extracts from the Sacred Record, bearing directly or indirectly on the subjects of purity and morality,—is therefore at once the most natural and the best.

In the case of a mere human work it might possibly be objected that the scope and intention of the whole could not fairly be gathered from a mere collection of extracts. Happily such an objection can have no weight here. Every verse, nay,

PREFACE.

every word of the Bible being the direct utterance or inspiration of the Most High, it necessarily follows that every portion of it is of equal authority. Consequently any particular passage may be, and in thousands of Churches every Sunday, is separated from the context without altering its meaning or impairing its force.

It may perhaps be urged that as all good Christians are thoroughly familiar with a book which has been their constant companion from early childhood, they must be already well acquainted with the passages here collected, or if not, that they could readily search them out for themselves. Many, however, have not the time or inclination to do this; and, in any case, many will be glad to have the passages brought together in a compact and convenient shape, so that their full force may be properly appreciated. To all such the present work will be a boon. Especially so will it be to the members of Young Men's and Young Women's Christian Associations, and to Sunday School children and their teachers. The works of Paine and Voltaire may not, it is true, be commonly found in the possession of children; while the Book whence the extracts here printed are taken, is, happily, in the hands of every young girl on her way to Church, and of every child on its way to Sunday School. Nevertheless, prevention is better than cure; and too great care cannot be exercised in guarding the young from contamination. Let but the receptive mind of a youth or maiden be once thoroughly imbued with the pure and perfect morality of the Bible, and the teachings of all the Paines and Voltaires in the world will be as harmless as a serpent's tooth is against a warrior clad in complete steel.

PREFACE.

The elucidation of the spotless purity and perfect morality of the Bible may be thought a work of supererogation, the task having been performed, or at least attempted, by so many commentators already. The Bible, however, has many aspects, and may be regarded from various standpoints ; and the aspect which it is here attempted to bring forcibly to the notice of orthodox Christians has been, if not absolutely ignored, at least unduly, not to say shamefully, neglected by them. It is hoped, then, that the present work may fill a void too long left unoccupied, and by supplementing, if not superseding, the more commonly received ideas, prove a contribution of some slight value towards arriving at a true estimate of the Christian Bible, its purity and morality.

The end in view has been sought to be obtained simply by the orderly selection, and the occasional juxtaposition, of passages from the Sacred Text itself. As Biblical truth shines with a light so refulgent of its own, it has been deemed unnecessary to add a single word of comment.

Toronto, November, 1881.

F. T. JONES.

CONTENTS.

		PAGE.
PART 1.	Passages illustrating the purity of the Holy Bible....................	9.
PART 2.	Passages illustrating the morality of the Holy Bible....................	53.

TO THE READER.

Where there are more passages than one between dashes, it is to be understood that they are to be read in connection with each other.

BIBLICAL ANTHOLOGY.

PART I.

Passages Illustrating the Purity of the Bible.

There were giants in the earth in those days; and also after that, when the sons of God came in unto the daughters of men, and they bare *children* to them.—Genesis VI. 4.

But Noah found grace in the eyes of the LORD. Noah was a just man *and* perfect in his generations, *and* Noah walked with God.—Genesis VI, 8-9.

And Noah began *to be* an husbandman, and he planted a vineyard. And he drank of the wine, and was drunken; and he was uncovered within his tent. And Ham, the father of Canaan, saw the nakedness of his father, and told his two brethren without.—Genesis IX, 20-22.

Now Sarai Abram's wife bare him no children: and she had an handmaid, an Egyptian, whose name *was* Hagar. And Sarai said unto Abram, Behold now, the LORD hath restrained me from bearing: I pray thee, go in unto my maid; it may be that I may obtain children by her. And Abram hearkened to the voice of Sarai. And Sarai Abram's wife took Hagar her maid the Egyptian, after Abram had dwelt ten years in the land of Canaan, and gave her to her husband Abram to be his wife.

And he went in unto Hagar, and she conceived.—Genesis XVI, 1-4.

And God said unto Abraham, Thou shall keep my covenant therefore, thou, and thy seed after thee in their generations. This *is* my covenant, which ye shall keep, between me and you and thy seed after thee; Every man child among you shall be circumcised. And ye shall circumcise the flesh of your foreskin; and it shall be a token of the covenant betwixt me and you. And he that is eight days old shall be circumcised among you, every man child in your generations, he that is born in the house, or bought with money of any stranger, which *is* not of thy seed. He that is born in thy house, and he that is bought with thy money, must needs be circumcised: and my covenant shall be in your flesh for an everlasting covenant. And the uncircumcised man child whose flesh of his foreskin is not circumcised, that soul shall be cut off from his people; he hath broken my covenant.

And Abraham took Ishmael his son, and all that were born in his house, and all that were bought with his money, every male among the men of Abraham's house; and circumcised the flesh of their foreskin in the selfsame day, as God had said unto him. And Abraham *was* ninety years old and nine, when he was circumcised in the flesh of his foreskin. And Ishmael his son *was* thirteen years old, when he was circumcised in the flesh of his foreskin. In the selfsame day was Abraham circumcised, and Ishmael his son. And all the men of his house, born in the house, and bought with money of the stranger, were circumcised with him.—Genesis XVII, 9-14, 23-27.

But before they lay down, the men of the city, *even* the men of Sodom, compassed the house around, both old and young, all the people from every quarter: And they called unto Lot, and said unto him, Where *are* the men which came in to thee this night? bring them out unto us, that we may know them. And Lot went out at the door unto them, and shut the door after him, And said, I pray you, brethren, do not so wickedly. Behold now, I have two daughters which have not known man; let me, I pray you, bring them out unto you, and do ye to them as *is* good in your eyes: only unto these men do nothing; for therefore came they under the shadow of my roof.—Genesis XIX, 4-8.

And Lot went up out of Zoar, and dwelt in the mountain, and his two daughters with him; for he feared to dwell in Zoar: and he dwelt in a cave, he and his two daughters. And the firstborn said unto the younger, Our father *is* old, and *there is* not a man in the earth to come in unto us after the manner of all the earth : Come, let us make our father drink wine, and we will lie with him, that we may preserve seed of our father. And they made their father drink wine that night: and the firstborn went in, and lay with her father; and he perceived not when she lay down, nor when she arose. And it came to pass on the morrow, that the firstborn said unto the younger, Behold, I lay yesternight with my father: let us make him drink wine this night also, and go thou in, *and* lie with him, that we may preserve the seed of our father. And they made their father drink wine that night also : and the younger arose, and lay with him; and he perceived not when she lay down, nor when she arose. Thus were both the daughters of Lot with child by their father. And the firstborn bare a son, and called his name Moab; the same *is* the father of the Moabites unto this day. And the younger, she also bare a son, and called his name Ben-ammi : the same *is* the father of the children of Ammon unto this day.—Genesis XIX, 30-38.

The LORD spake unto me, saying, Thou art to pass over through Ar, the coast of Moab, this day : And *when* thou comest nigh over against the children of Ammon, distress them not, nor meddle with them : for I will not give thee of the land of the children of Ammon *any* possessions ; because I have given it unto the children of Lot *for* a possession.—Deuteronomy II, 17-19.

And Isaac intreated the LORD for his wife, because she *was* barren : and the LORD was intreated of him, and Rebekah his wife conceived. And the children struggled together within her; and she said, If *it* be so, why *am* I thus? And she went to enquire of the LORD. And the LORD said unto her, Two nations *are* in thy womb, and two manner of people shall be separated from thy bowels ; and *the one* people shall be stronger than *the other* people ; and the elder shall serve the younger.

And when her days to be delivered were fulfilled, behold, *there were* twins in her womb. And the first came out red, all over like an hairy garment; and they called his name Esau. And after that came his brother out, and his hands took hold on Esau's heel; and his name was called Jacob : and Isaac *was* three-score years old when she bare them.—Genesis xxv, 21-26.

And when Rachel saw that she bare Jacob no children, Rachel envied her sister; and said unto Jacob, Give me children, or else I die. And Jacob's anger was kindled against Rachel: and he said, *Am* I in God's stead, who hath withheld from thee the fruit of the womb? And she said, Behold my maid Bilhah, go in unto to her; and she shall bear upon my knees, that I may also have children by her. And she gave him Bilhah her handmaid to wife : and Jacob went in unto her. And Bilhah conceived and bare Jacob a son. And Rachel said, God hath judged me, and hath also heard my voice, and hath given me a son: therefore called she his name Dan. And Bilhah Rachel's maid conceived again, and bare Jacob a second son. And Rachel said, With great wrestlings have I wrestled with my sister, and I have prevailed : and she called his name Naphtali.

When Leah saw that she had left bearing, she took Zilpah her maid and gave her Jacob to wife. And Zilpah Leah's maid bare Jacob a son. And Leah said, A troop cometh : and she called his name Gad. And Zilpah Leah's maid bare Jacob a second son. And Leah said, Happy am I, for the daughters will call me blessed : and she called his name Asher.

And Reuben went in the days of wheat harvest, and found mandrakes in the field, and brought them unto his mother Leah. Then Rachel said to Leah, Give me, I pray thee, of thy son's mandrakes. And she said unto her, *Is it* a small matter that thou hast taken my husband? and wouldest thou take away my son's mandrakes also? And Rachel said, Therefore he shall lie with thee to night for thy son's mandrakes. And Jacob came out of the field in the evening, and Leah went out to meet him, and said, Thou must come in unto me ; for surely I have hired thee with my son's mandrakes. And he lay with her that night. And God hearkened unto Leah, and she conceived, and bare Jacob the fifth son. And Leah said, God hath given me my hire, because I have given my maiden to my husband; and she called his name Issachar. And Leah conceived again, and bare Jacob the sixth son. And Leah said, God hath endued me *with* a good dowry; now will my husband dwell with me, because I have born him six sons: and she called his name Zebulun. And afterwards she bare a daughter, and called her name Dinah.

And God remembered Rachel, and God hearkened to her, and opened her womb. And she conceived, and bare a son; and said, God hath taken away my reproach: And she called his name Joseph; and said, The LORD shall add to me another son.—Genesis XXX, 1-24.

And Laban went into Jacob's tent, and into Leah's tent, and into the two maidservants' tent; but he found *them* not. Then went he out of Leah's tent, and entered into Rachel's tent. Now Rachel had taken the images, and put them in the camel's furniture, and sat upon them. And Laban searched all the tent, but found *them* not. And she said to her father, Let it not displease my lord that I cannot rise up before thee; for the custom of women *is* upon me. And he searched, but found not the images.—Genesis XXXI, 33-35.

And Dinah the daughter of Leah, which she bare unto Jacob, went out to see the daughters of the land. And when Shechem the son of Hamor the Hivite, prince of the country, saw her, he took her, and lay with her, and defiled her.—Genesis XXXIV, 1-2.

And it came to pass, when Israel dwelt in that land, that Reuben went and lay with Bilhah his father's concubine: and Israel heard *it*.—Genesis XXXV, 22.

And it came to pass at that time, that Judah went down from his brethren, and turned in to a certain Adullamite, whose name *was* Hirah. And Judah saw there a daughter of a certain Canaanite, whose name was Shuah ; and he took her, and went in unto her. And she conceived, and bare a son ; and he called his name Er. And she conceived again, and bare a son ; and she called his name Onan. And she yet again conceived, and bare a son ; and called his name Shelah : and he was at Chezib, when she bare him.

And Judah took a wife for Er his firstborn, whose name was Tamar. And Er, Judah's firstborn, was wicked in the sight of the LORD ; and the LORD slew him. And Judah said unto Onan, Go in unto thy brother's wife, and marry her, and raise up seed to thy brother. And Onan knew that the seed should not be his ; and it came to pass, when he went in unto his brother's wife, that he spilled it on the ground, lest that it should give seed to his brother. And the thing which he did displeased the LORD ; wherefore he slew him also.

Then said Judah to Tamar his daughter in law, Remain a widow at thy father's house, till Shelah my son be grown : for he said, Lest peradventure he die also, as his brethren did. And Tamar went and dwelt in her father's house.

And in process of time the daughter of Shuah Judah's wife died ; and Judah was comforted, and went up unto his sheepshearers to Timnath, he and his friend Hirah the Adullamite. And it was told Tamar, saying, Behold thy father in law goeth up to Timnath to shear his sheep. And she put her widow's garments off from her, and covered her with a vail, and wrapped herself, and sat in an open place, which is by the way to Timnath ; for she saw that Shelah was grown, and she was not given unto him to wife. When Judah saw her, he thought her to be an harlot ; because she had covered her face. And he turned unto her by the way, and said, Go to, I pray thee, let me come in unto thee ; (for he knew not that she was his daughter in law.) And she said, What wilt thou give me, that thou mayest come in unto me ? And he said, I will send thee a kid from the flock. And she said, Wilt thou give me a pledge, till thou send it ? And he said, What pledge shall I give thee ? And she said, Thy signet, and thy bracelets, and thy staff that is in thine hand. And he gave it her, and came in unto her, and she conceived by him.

And she arose, and went away, and laid by her vail from her, and put on the garments of her widowhood. And Judah sent the kid by the hand of his friend the Adullamite, to receive *his* pledge from the woman's hand; but he found her not. Then he asked the men of that place, saying, Where *is* the harlot, that *was* openly by the way side? And they said, There was no harlot in this *place*. And he returned to Judah, and said, I cannot find her; and also the men of the place said, *that* there was no harlot in this *place*. And Judah said, Let her take *it* to her, lest we be ashamed: behold, I send this kid, and thou hast not found her.

And it came to pass about three months after, that it was told Judah, saying, Tamar thy daughter in law hath played the harlot; and also, behold, she *is* with child by whoredom. And Judah said, Bring her forth, and let her be burnt. When she *was* brought forth, she sent to her father in law, saying, By the man, whose these *are*, *am* I with child: and she said, Discern, I pray thee, whose *are* these, the signet, and bracelets, and staff. And Judah acknowledged *them*, and said, She hath been more righteous than I; because that I gave her not to Shelah my son. And he knew her again no more.

And it came to pass in the of time her travail, that, behold, twins *were* in her womb. And it came to pass, when she travailed, that *the one* put out *his* hand: and the midwife took and bound upon *his* hand a scarlet thread, saying This came out first. And it came to pass, as he drew back his hand, that, behold, his brother came out: and she said, How hast thou broken forth? *this* breach *be* upon thee, therefore his name was called Pharez. And afterward came out his brother, that had the scarlet thread upon his hand: and his name was called Zarah.—Genesis xxxviii, 1-30.

And it came to pass after these things, that his master's wife cast her eyes upon Joseph; and she said, Lie with me. But he refused, and said unto his master's wife, Behold, my master wotteth not what *is* with me in the house, and he hath committed all that he hath to my hand; *There* is none greater in this house than I; neither hath he kept back anything from me but thee, because thou *art* his wife: how then can I do this great wickedness, and sin against God? And it came to pass, as she spake to Joseph day by day, that he hearkened not unto her, to lie by her, *or* to be with her. And it came to pass about this time, that *Joseph* went into the house to do his business; and *there was* none of the men of the house there within. And she caught him by his garment, saying, Lie with me: and he left his garment in her hand, and fled, and got him out. And it came to pass, when she saw he had left his garment in her hand, and was fled forth, That she called unto the men of her house, and spake unto them, saying, See, he hath brought in an Hebrew unto us to mock us; he came in unto me to lie with me, and I cried with a loud voice: And it came to pass, when he heard that I lifted up my voice and cried, that he left his garment with me, and fled, and got him out. And she laid up his garment by her, until his lord came home.

And she spake unto him according to these words, saying, The Hebrew servant, which thou hast brought unto us, came in unto me to mock me: And it came to pass, as I lifted up my voice and cried, that he left his garment with me, and fled out. And it came to pass, when his master heard the words of his wife, which she spake unto him, saying, After this manner did thy servant to me; that his wrath was kindled. And Joseph's master took him, and put him into the prison, a place where the king's prisoners *were* bound: and he was there in the prison.—Genesis xxxix, 7-20.

Reuben, thou *art* my firstborn, my might, and the beginning of my strength, the excellency of dignity, and the excellency of power: Unstable as water, thou shalt not excel; because thou wentest up to thy father's bed; then defiledst thou *it*; he went up to my couch. Genesis xlix, 3-4.

And the King of Egypt spake to the Hebrew midwives, of which the name of the one *was* Shiphrah, and the name of the other Puah: And he said, When ye do the office of a midwife to the Hebrew women, and see *them* upon the stools; if it *be* a son, then ye shall kill him: but if it *be* a daughter. then she shall live. But the midwives feared God, and did not as the king of Egypt commanded them, but saved the men children alive. And the king of Egypt called for the midwives, and said unto them, Why have ye done this thing, and have saved the men children alive? And the midwives said unto Pharaoh, Because the Hebrew women *are* not as the Egyptian women; for they *are* lively, and are delivered ere the midwives come in unto them.—Exodus I, 15-21.

And it came to pass by the way in the inn, that the LORD met him, and sought to kill him. Then Zipporah took a sharp stone, and cut off the foreskin of her son, and cast *it* at his feet, and said, Surely a bloody husband *art* thou to me. So he let him go: then she said, A bloody husband *thou art*, because of the circumcision.—Exodus IV, 24-26.

And if a man entice a maid that is not betrothed, and lie with her, he shall surely endow her to be his wife. If her father utterly refuse to give her unto him, he shall pay money according to the dowry of virgins.

Thou shalt not suffer a witch to live.

Whosoever lieth with a beast shall surely be put to death.—Exodus XXII, 16-19.

And the LORD said, Behold, *there is* a place by me, and thou shalt stand upon a rock: And it shall come to pass, while my glory passeth by, that I will put thee in a clift of the rock, and will cover thee with my hand while I pass by: And I will take away mine hand, and thou shalt see my back parts: but my face shall not be seen.—Exodus XXXIII, 21-23.

And the LORD spake unto Moses, saying, Speak unto the children of Israel, saying, If a woman have conceived seed, and born a man child: then she shall be unclean seven days; according to the days of the separation for her infirmity shall she be unclean. And in the eighth day the flesh of his foreskin shall be circumcised. And she shall then continue in the blood of her purifying three and thirty days; she shall touch no hallowed thing, nor come into the sanctuary, until the days of her purifying be fulfilled. But if she bear a maid child, then she shall be unclean two weeks, as in her separation: and she shall continue in the blood of her purifying threescore and six days. And when the days of her purifying are fulfilled, for a son, or for a daughter, she shall bring a lamb of the first year for a burnt offering, and a young pigeon, or a turtledove, for a sin offering, unto the door of the tabernacle of the congregation, unto the priest, Who shall offer it before the LORD, and make an atouement for her? and she shall be cleansed from the issue of her blood. This *is* the law for her that hath born a male or a female. And if she be not able to bring a lamb, then she shall bring two turtles, or two young pigeons; the one for the burnt offering, and the other for a sin offering: and the priest shall make an atouement for her, and she shall be clean.—Leviticus XII, 1-8.

And the LORD spake unto Moses and to Aaron, saying, Speak unto the children of Israel, and say unto them, When any man hath a running issue out of his flesh, *because of* his issue he *is* unclean. And this shall be his uncleanness in his issue: whether his flesh run with his issue, or his flesh be stopped from his issue, it *is* his uncleanness. Every bed, whereon he lieth that hath the issue, is unclean: and every thing, whereon he sitteth, shall be unclean. And whosoever toucheth his bed shall wash his clothes, and bathe *himself* in water, and be unclean until the even. And he that sitteth on *any* thing whereon he sat that hath the issue shall wash his clothes, and bathe himself in water, and be unclean until the even. And he that toucheth the flesh of him that hath the issue shall wash his clothes, and bathe *himself* in water, and be unclean until the even. And if he that hath the issue spit upon him that is clean; then he shall wash his clothes, and bathe *himself* in water, and be unclean until the even. And what saddle soever he rideth upon that hath the issue shall be unclean. And whosoever toucheth anything that was under

BIBLICAL ANTHOLOGY. 19

him shall be unclean until the even: and he that beareth *any of* those things shall wash his clothes, and bathe *himself* in water, and be unclean until the even. And whomsoever he toucheth that hath the issue, and hath not rinsed his hands in water, he shall wash his clothes, and bathe *himself* in water, and be unclean until the even. And the vessel of earth, that he touched which hath the issue, shall be broken: and every vessel of wood shall be rinsed in water. And when he that hath an issue is cleansed of his issue; then he shall number to himself seven days for his cleansing, and wash his clothes, and bathe his flesh in running water, and shall be clean.—Leviticus xv, 1-13.

And if any man's seed of copulation go out from him, then he shall wash all his flesh in water, and be unclean until the even. And every garment, and every skin, whereon is the seed of copulation, shall be washed with water, and be unclean until the even. The woman also with whom man shall lie *with* seed of copulation, they shall *both* bathe *themselves* in water and be unclean until the even.

And if a woman have an issue, *and* her issue in her flesh be blood, she shall be put apart seven days : and whosoever toucheth her shall be unclean until the even. And every thing that she lieth upon in her separation shall be unclean : every thing also that she sitteth upon shall be unclean. And whosoever toucheth her bed shall wash his clothes, and bathe *himself* in water, and be unclean until the even. And whosoever toucheth any thing that she sat upon shall wash his clothes, and bathe *himself* in water, and be unclean until the even. And if it *be* on *her* bed, or on anything whereon she sitteth, when he toucheth it, he shall be unclean until the even. And if any man lie with her at all, and her flowers be upon him, he shall be unclean seven days ; and all the bed whereon he lieth shall be unclean. And if a woman have an issue of her blood many days out of the time of her separation, or if it run beyond the time of her separation ; all the days of the issue of her uncleanness shall be as the days of her separation : she *shall be* unclean. Every bed whereon she lieth all the days of her issue shall be unto her as the bed of her separation :

and whatsoever she sitteth upon shall be unclean, as the uncleanness of her separation. And whosoever toucheth those things shall be unclean, and shall wash his clothes, and bathe *himself* in water, and be unclean until the even. But if she be cleansed of her issue, then she shall number to herself seven days, and after that she shall be clean. And on the eighth day she shall take unto her two turtles, or two young pigeons, and bring them unto the priest, to the door of the tabernacle of the congregation. And the priest shall offer the one *for* a sin offering, and the other *for* a burnt offering; and the priest shall make an atonement for her before the LORD for the issue of her uncleanness. Thus shall ye separate the children of Israel from their uncleanness; that they die not in their uncleanness, when they defile my tabernacle that *is* among them.

This *is* the law of him that hath an issue, and *of him* whose seed goeth from him, and is defiled therewith; And of her that is sick of her flowers, and of him that hath an issue, of the man, and of the woman, and of him that lieth with her that is unclean.—Leviticus xv, 16-33.

———

None of you shall approach to any that is near of kin to him, to uncover *their* nakedness: I *am* the LORD. The nakedness of thy father, or the nakedness of thy mother, shalt thou not uncover: she *is* thy mother; thou shalt not uncover her nakedness. The nakedness of thy father's wife shalt thou not uncover: it *is* thy father's nakedness. The nakedness of thy sister, the daughter of thy father, or daughter of thy mother, *whether she be* born at home, or born abroad, *even* their nakedness thou shalt not uncover. The nakedness of thy son's daughter, or of thy daughter's daughter, *even* their nakedness thou shalt not uncover: for their's is thine own nakedness. The nakedness of thy father's wife's daughter, begotten of thy father, she *is* thy sister, thou shalt not uncover her nakedness. Thou shalt not uncover the nakedness of thy father's sister: she *is* thy father's near kinswoman. Thou shalt not uncover the nakedness of thy mother's sister: for she *is* thy mother's near kinswoman. Thou shalt not uncover the nakedness of thy father's brother, thou shalt not approach to his

BIBLICAL ANTHOLOGY.

wife : she *is* thine aunt. Thou shalt not uncover the nakedness of thy daughter in law :' she *is* thy son's wife ; thou shalt not uncover her nakedness. Thou shalt not uncover the nakedness of thy brother's wife ; it *is* thy brother's nakedness. Thou shalt not uncover the nakedness of a woman and her daughter, neither shalt thou take her son's daughter, or her daughter's daughter, to uncover her nakedness ; *for* they *are* her near kinswomen : it *is* wickedness. Neither shalt thou take a wife to her sister to vex *her*, to uncover her nakedness, beside the other in her life *time*. Also thou shalt not approach unto a woman to uncover her nakedness, as long as she is put apart for her uncleanness. Moreover thou shalt not lie carnally with thy neighbour's wife, to defile thyself with her. And thou shalt not let any of thy seed pass through *the fire* to Molech, neither shalt thou profane the name of thy God : I *am* the LORD. Thou shalt not lie with mankind, as with womankind : it *is* abomination. Neither shalt thou lie with any beast to defile thyself therewith : neither shall any woman stand before a beast to lie down therein : it *is* confusion.—Leviticus XVIII, 6-23.

And the man that committeth adultery with *another* man's wife, *even he* that committeth adultery with his neighbour's wife, the adulterer and the adulteress shall surely be put to death. And the man that lieth with his father's wife hath uncovered his father's nakedness : both of them shall surely be put to death ; their blood *shall be* upon them. And if a man lie with his daughter in law, both of them shall surely be put to death : they have wrought confusion ; their blood *shall be* upon them. If a man also lie with mankind, as he lieth with a woman, both of them have committed an abomination: they shall surely be put to death ; their blood *shall be* upon them. And if a man take a wife and her mother, it *is* wickedness : they shall be burnt with fire, both he and they ; that there be no wickedness among you. And if a man lie with a beast, he shall surely be put to death ; and ye shall slay the beast. And if a woman approach unto any beast, and lie down thereto, thou shalt kill the woman, and the beast ; they shall surely be put to death ; their blood *shall be* upon them. And if a man shall take his sister, his father's daughter, or his mother's daughter, and see her nakedness, and she see his nakedness ; it is a wicked thing ; and they shall be cut off in the sight of their people : he hath uncovered his sister's nakedness ; he shall bear his iniquity. And if a man shall lie with a woman having her sickness, and shall uncover her nakedness ; he hath discovered her fountain, and she hath uncovered the fountain of her blood : and both of them shall be cut off from among their people. And thou shalt not uncover the nakedness of thy mother's sister, nor of thy father's sister : for he uncovereth his near kin : they shall bear their iniquity. And if a man shall lie with his uncle's wife, he hath uncovered his uncle's nakedness : they shall bear their sin ; they shall die childless. And if a man shall take his brother's wife, it *is* an unclean thing : he hath uncovered his brother's nakedness ; they shall be childless.—Leviticus xx, 10-21.

And the LORD spake unto Moses, saying. Speak unto the children of Israel, and say unto them, If any man's wife go aside, and commit a trespass against him, And a man lie with her carnally, and it be hid from the eyes of the husband, and be kept close, and she be defiled, and *there be* no witness against her, neither she be taken *with the manner;* And the spirit of jealousy come upon him, and he be jealous of his wife, and she be defiled: or if the spirit of jealousy come upon him, and he be jealous of his wife, and she be not defiled: Then shall the man bring his wife unto the priest, and he shall bring her offering for her, the tenth *part* of an ephah of barley meal ; he shall pour no oil upon it, nor put frankincense thereon ; for it *is* an offering of jealousy, an offering of memorial, bringing iniquity to remembrance.

And the priest shall bring her near, and set her before the LORD: And the priest shall take holy water in an earthen vessel; and of the dust that is in the floor of the tabernacle the priest shall take, and put *it* into the water: And the priest shall set the woman before the LORD, and uncover the woman's head, and put the offering of memorial in her hands, which *is* the jealousy offering: and the priest

BIBLICAL ANTHOLOGY.

shall have in his hand the bitter water that causeth the curse: And the priest shall charge her by an oath, and say unto the woman, If no man have lain with thee, and if thou hast not gone aside to uncleanness *with another* instead of thy husband, be thou free from this bitter water that causeth the curse: But if thou hast gone aside *to another* instead of thy husband, and if thou be defiled, and some man have lain with thee beside thine husband: Then the priest shall charge the woman with an oath of cursing, and the priest shall say unto the woman, The LORD make thee a curse and an oath among thy people, when the LORD doth make thy thigh to rot, and thy belly to swell; And this water that causeth the curse shall go into thy bowels, to make *thy* belly to swell, and *thy* thigh to rot: And the woman shall say, Amen, amen.

And the priest shall write three curses in a book, and he shall blot *them* out with the bitter water: And he shall cause the woman to drink the bitter water that causeth the curse: and the water that causeth the curse shall enter into her, *and become* bitter. Then the priest shall take the jealousy offering out of the woman's hand, and shall wave the offering before the LORD, and offer it upon the altar: And the priest shall take an handful of the offering, *even* the memorial thereof, and burn *it* upon the altar, and afterwards shall cause the woman to drink the water.

And when he hath made her to drink the water, then it shall come to pass, *that*, if she be defiled, and have done trespa s against her husband, that the water that causeth the curse shall enter into her, *and become* bitter, and her belly shall swell, and her thigh shall rot: and the woman shall be a curse among her people. And if the woman be not defiled, but be clean; then she shall be free, and shall conceive seed.

This *is* the law of jealousies, when a wife goeth aside *to another* instead of her husband, and is defiled.—Numbers v, 11-29.

Now the man Moses *was* very meek, above all the men which *were* upon the face of the earth.—Numbers XII, 3.

And they warred against the Midianites, as the LORD commanded Moses; and they slew all the males. And they slew the kings of Midian, beside the rest of them that were slain; *namely*, Evi, and Rekem, and Zur, and Hur, and Reba, five kings of Midian; Balaam also the son of Beor they slew with the sword. And the children of Israel took *all* the women of Midian captives, and their little ones, and took the spoil of all their cattle, and all their flocks, and all their goods. And they burnt all their cities wherein they dwelt, and all their goodly castles, with fire. And they took all the spoil, and all the prey, *both* of men and of beasts. And they brought the captives, and the prey, and the spoil, unto Moses, and Eleazar the priest, and unto the congregation of the children of Israel, unto the camp at the plains of Moab, which *are* by Jordan *near* Jericho.

And Moses, and Eleazar the priest, and all the princes of the congregation, went forth to meet them without the camp. And Moses was wroth with the officers of the host, *with* the captains over thousands, and captains over hundreds, which came from the battle. And Moses said unto them, Have ye saved all the women alive? Behold, these caused the children of Israel, through the counsel of Balaam, to commit trespass against the LORD in the matter of Peor, and there was a plague among the congregation of the LORD. Now therefore kill every male among the little ones, and kill every woman that hath known man by lying with him. But all the women children, that have not known a man by lying with him, keep alive for yourselves.—Numbers XXXI, 7-18.

And there arose not a prophet since in Israel like unto Moses, whom the LORD knew face to face.—Deuteronomy XXXIV, 10.

When thou goest forth to war against thine enemies, and the LORD thy God hath delivered them into thine hands, and thou hast taken them captive, And seest among the captives a beautiful woman, and hast a desire unto her, that thou wouldest have her to thy wife; Then thou shalt bring her home to thine house; and she shall shave her head, and pare her nails; And she shall put the raiment of her

captivity from off her, and shall remain in thine house, and bewail her father and her mother a full month: and after that thou shalt go in unto her, and be her husband, and she shall be thy wife. And it shall be, if thou have no delight in her, then thou shalt let her go whither she will; but thou shalt not sell her at all for money, thou shalt not make merchandise of her, because thou hast humbled her.
—Deuteronomy XXI, 10-14.

If any man take a wife, and go in unto her, and hate her, And give occasions of speech against her, and bring up an evil name upon her, and say, I took this woman, and when I came to her, I found her not a maid : Then shall the father of the damsel, and her mother, take and bring forth *the tokens of* the damsel's virginity unto the elders of the city in the gate : And the damsel's father shall say unto the elders, I gave my daughter unto this man to wife, and he hateth her ; And, lo, he hath given occasions of speech *against her*, saying, I found not thy daughter a maid ; and yet these *are the tokens of* my daughter's virginity. And they shall spread the cloth before the elders of the city. And the elders of that city shall take that man and chastise him ; And they shall amerce him in an hundred *shekels* of silver, and give *them* unto the father of the damsel, because he hath brought up an evil name upon a virgin of Israel : and she shall be his wife ; he may not put her away all his days.

But if this thing be true, *and the tokens of* virginity be not found for the damsel : Then they shall bring out the damsel to the door of her father's house, and the men of her city shall stone her with stones that she die : because she hath wrought folly in Israel, to play the whore in her father's house : so shalt thou put evil away from among you.

If a man be found lying with a woman married to an husband, then they shall both of them die, *both* the man that lay with the woman, and the woman : so shalt thou put away evil from Israel.

If a damsel *that is* a virgin be betrothed unto an husband, and a man find her in the city, and lie with her ; Then ye shall bring them both out unto the gate of that city, and ye shall stone them with stones that they die; the damsel, because she cried not, *being* in the city; and the man, because he hath humbled his neighbour's wife; so thou shalt put away evil from among you.

But if a man find a betrothed damsel in the field, and the man force her, and lie with her : then the man only that lay with her shall die : But unto the damsel thou shalt do nothing; *there* is in the damsel no sin *worthy* of death; for as when a man riseth against his neighbour, and slayeth him, even so *is* this matter : For he found her in the field, *and* the betrothed damsel cried, and there *was* none to save her.

If a man find a damsel *that is* a virgin, which is not betrothed, and lay hold on her, and lie with her, and they be found; then the man that lay with her shall give unto the damsel's father fifty *shekels* of silver, and she shall be his wife; because he hath humbled her, he may not put her away all his days.

A man shall not take his father's wife, nor discover his father's skirt.—Deuteronomy xxii, 13-30.

He that is wounded in the stones, or hath his privy member cut off, shall not enter into the congregation of the LORD. A bastard shall not enter into the congregation of the LORD; even to his tenth generation shall he not enter into the congregation of the LORD. —Deuteronomy xxiii, 1-2.

If there be among you any man, that is not clean by reason of uncleanness that chanceth him by night, then shall he go abroad out of the camp, he shall not come within the camp : But it shall be, when evening cometh on, he shall wash *himself* with water : and when the sun is down, he shall come into the camp *again.*

Thou shalt have a place also without the camp, whither thou shalt go forth abroad : And thou shalt have a paddle upon thy weapon; and it shall be, when thou wilt ease thyself abroad, thou shalt dig therewith, and shalt turn back and cover that which cometh from thee.—Deuteronomy xxiii, 10-13.

When men strive together, one with another, and the wife of the one draweth near for to deliver her husband out of the hand of him that smiteth him, and putteth forth her hand and taketh him by the secrets : Then thou shalt cut off her hand, thine eye shall not pity her.—Deuteronomy xxv, 11-12.

Cursed be he that lieth with his father's wife ; because he uncovereth his father's skirt, And all the people shall say, Amen. Cursed be he that lieth with any manner of beast. And all the people shall say, Amen. Cursed be he that lieth with his sister, the daughter of his father, or the daughter of his mother. And all the people shall say, Amen. Cursed be he that lieth with his mother in law. And all the people shall say, Amen.—Deuteronomy xxvii, 20-23.

At that time the LORD said unto Joshua, Make thee sharp knives, and circumcise again the children of Israel the second time. And Joshua made him sharp knives, and circumcised the children of Israel at the hill of the foreskins.—Joshua v, 2-3.

And Ehud put forth his left hand, and took the dagger from his right thigh, and thrust it into his belly : And the haft also went in after the blade ; and the fat closed upon the blade, so that he could not draw the dagger out of his belly ; and the dirt came out. —Judges iii, 21-22.

But it came to pass within a while after, in the time of the wheat harvest, that Sampson visited his wife with a kid ; and he said, I will go in to my wife into the chamber. But her father would not suffer him to go in. And her father said, I verily thought that thou hadst utterly hated her ; therefore I gave her to thy companion : is not her youngest sister fairer than she ? take her, I pray thee, instead of her.—Judges xv, 1-2.

Then went Sampson to Gaza and saw there an harlot, and went in unto her.—Judges xvi, 1.

Now as they were making their hearts merry, behold, the men of the city, certain sons of Belial, beset the house round about, *and* beat at the door, and spake to the master of the house, the old man, saying, Bring forth the man that came into thine house, that we may know him. And the man, the master of the house, went out unto them, and said unto them, Nay, my brethren, *nay*, I pray you, do not *so* wickedly; seeing that this man is come into mine house, do not this folly. Behold, *here* is my daughter a maiden, and his concubine: them I will bring out now, and humble ye them, and do with them what seemeth good unto you: but unto this man do not so vile a thing. But the men would not hearken to him: so the man took his concubine, and brought her forth unto them; and they knew her, and abused her all the night until the morning: and when the day began to spring, they let her go. Then came the woman in the dawning of the day, and fell down at the door of the man's house, and her hands *were* upon the threshold. And he said unto her, Up, and let us be going. But none answered. Then the man took her *up* upon an ass, and the man rose up, and gat him unto his place.

And when he was come into his house, he took a knife, and laid hold on his concubine, and divided her, *together* with her bones, into twelve pieces, and sent her into all the coasts of Israel.—Judges xix, 22-29.

Then Naomi her mother in law said unto her, My daughter, shall I not seek rest for thee, that it may be well with thee! And now *is* not Boaz of our kindred, with whose maidens thou wast? Behold he winnoweth barley to-night in the threshingfloor. Wash thyself therefore, and anoint thee, and put thy raiment upon thee, and get thee down to the floor: *but* make not thyself known unto the man, until he shall have done eating and drinking. And it shall be, when he lieth down, that thou shalt mark the place where he shall lie, and thou shalt go in and uncover his feet, and lay thee down; and he will tell thee what thou shalt do. And she said unto her, All that thou sayest unto me I will do.

And she went down unto the floor, and did according to all that her mother in law bade her. And when Boaz had eaten and drunk, and his heart was merry, he went to lie down at the end of the heap of corn : and she came softly, and uncovered his feet, and laid her down.

And it came to pass at midnight, that the man was afraid, and turned himself : and, behold, a woman lay at his feet. And he said, Who *art* thou? And she answered, I *am* Ruth thine handmaid : spread therefore thy skirt over thine handmaid ; for thou *art* a near kinsman. And he said, Blessed *be* thou of the LORD, my daughter : for thou hast shewed more kindness in the latter end than at the beginning, inasmuch as thou followedst not young men, whether poor or rich. And now, my daughter, fear not ; I will do to thee all that thou requirest : for all the city of my people doth know that thou *art* a virtuous woman. And now it is true that I *am thy* near kinsman : howbeit there is a kinsman nearer than I. Tarry this night, and it shall be in the *morning*, that if he will perform unto thee the part of a kinsman, well ; let him do the kinsman's part : but if he will not do the part of a kinsman to thee, then will I do the part of a kinsman to thee, *as* the LORD liveth : lie down until the morning.

And she lay at his feet until the morning : and she rose up before one could know another. And he said, Let it not be known that a woman came into the floor. Also he said, Bring the vail that *thou hast* upon thee, and hold it. And when she held it, he measured six *measures* of barley, and laid *it* on her : and she went into the city. And when she came to her mother in law, she said, Who *art* thou, my daughter ? And she told her all that the man had done to her. And she said, These six *measures* of barley gave he me; for he said to me, Go not empty unto thy mother in law. Then said she, Sit still, my daughter, until thou know how the matter will fall : for the man will not be in rest, until he have finished the thing this day.—Ruth III, 1-18.

Now Eli was very old, and heard all that his sons did unto all Israel ; and how they lay with the women that assembled *at* the door of the tabernacle of the congregation.—1 Samuel II, 22.

And it was *so*, that, after they had carried it about, the hand of the LORD was against the city with a very great destruction : and he smote the men of the city, both small and great, and they had emerods * in their secret parts.—1 Samuel v, 9.

And Saul said, Thus shall ye say to David, The king desireth not any dowry, but an hundred foreskins of the Philistines, to be avenged of the king's enemies. But Saul thought to make David fall by the hand of the Philistines. And when his servants told David these words, it pleased David well to be the king's son in law : and the days were not expired. Wherefore David arose and went, he and his men, and slew of the Philistines two hundred men ; and David brought their foreskins, and they gave them in full tale to the king that he might be the king's son in law. And Saul gave him Michal his daughter to wife.—1 Samuel XVIII, 25-27.

And the priest answered David, and said, *There* is no common bread under mine hand, but there is hallowed bread ; if the young men have kept themselves at least from women. And David answered the priest, and said unto him, Of a truth women *have been* kept from us about these three days, since I came out, and the vessels of the young men are holy, and the *bread is* in a manner common, yea, though it were sanctified this day in the vessel.—1 Samuel, XXI, 4-5.

So and more also do God unto the enemies of David, if I leave of all that *pertain* to him by the morning light any that pisseth against the wall.

For in the very deed, *as* the LORD God of Israel liveth, which hath kept me back from hurting thee, except thou hadst hasted and come to meet me, surely there had not been left unto Nabal by the morning light any that pisseth against the wall.—1 Samuel XXV, 22, 34.

---

* "EMERODS, that is hemorroids, the name of a painful disease occasioned by tumours, probably the piles."—Rand's Bible Dictionary.

BIBLICAL ANTHOLOGY. 31

And David danced before the LORD with all *his* might ; and David was girded with a linen ephod. *
And as the ark of the LORD came into the city of David, Michal Saul's daughter looked through a window, and saw King David leaping and dancing before the LORD ; and she despised him in her heart.
Then David returned to bless his household. And Michal, the daughter of Saul, came out to meet David, and said, How glorious was the king of Israel to day, who uncovered himself to day in the eyes of the handmaids of his servants, as one of the vain fellows shamelessly uncovereth himself ! And David said unto Michal, *It was* before the LORD, which chose me before thy father, and before all his house, to appoint me ruler over the people of the LORD, over Israel : therefore will I play before the LORD. And I will yet be more vile than thus, and will be base in mine own sight : and of the maidservants which thou hast spoken of, of them shall I be had in honour. Therefore Michal the daughter of Saul had no child unto the day of her death.—2 Samuel VI, 14, 16, 20-23.

And it came to pass in an eveningtide, that David arose from off his bed, and walked upon the roof of the king's house : and from the roof he saw a woman washing herself ; and the woman was very beautiful to look upon. And David sent and enquired after the woman. And *one* said, *Is* not this Bath-sheba, the daughter of Eliam, the wife of Uriah the Hittite ? And David sent messengers, and took her ; and she came in unto him, and he lay with her ; for she was purified from her uncleanness : and she returned unto her house. And the woman conceived and sent and told David, and said, I *am* with child.—2 Samuel XI, 2-5.

I have found David, the *son* of Jesse, a man after mine own heart, which shall fulfil all my will.—Acts XIII, 22.

---
* " EPHOD, an ornamental part of the dress worn by the Hebrew priests. It was, without sleeves, and open below the arms on each side, consisting of two pieces, one of which covered the front of the body and the other the back, joined together on the shoulders, and reaching down to the middle of the thigh."—Rand's Bible Dictionary.

Thus saith the LORD, Behold, I will raise up evil against thee out of thine own house, and I will take thy wives before thine eyes and give them unto thy neighbour, and he shall lie with thy wives in the sight of this sun.—2 Samuel XII, 11.

And it came to pass after this, that Absalom the son of David had a fair sister, whose name *was* Tamar ; and Amnon the son of David loved her. And Amnon was so vexed, that he fell sick for his sister Tamar ; for she was a virgin ; and Amnon thought it hard for him to do anything to her. But Amnon had a friend, whose name *was* Jonadab, the son of Shimeah, David's brother : and Jonadab was a very subtil man. And he said unto him, Why *art* thou, *being* the king's son, lean from day to day ? wilt thou not tell me ? And Amnon said unto him, I love Tamar, my brother Absalom's sister. And Jonadab said unto him, Lay thee down on thy bed, and make thyself sick : and when thy father cometh to see thee, say unto him, I pray thee, let my sister Tamar come, and give me meat, and dress the meat in my sight, that I may see *it*, and eat *it* at her hand.

So Amnon lay down, and ma le himself sick : and when the king was come to see him, Amnon said unto the king, I pray thee, let Tamar my sister come, and make me a couple of cakes in my sight, that I may eat at her hand. Then David sent home to Tamar, saying, Go now to thy brother Amnon's house, and dress him meat.

So Tamar went to her brother Amnon's house ; and he was laid down. And she took flour and kneaded *it*, and made cakes in his sight, and did bake the cakes. And she took a pan, and poured *them* out before him ; but he refused to eat. And Amnon said, Have out all men from me. And they went out every man from him. And Amnon said unto Tamar, Bring the meat into the chamber, that I may eat of thine hand. And Tamar took the cakes which she had made, and brought *them* into the chamber to Amnon her brother. And when she had brought *them* unto him to eat, he took hold of her, and said unto her, Come lie with me, my sister. And she answered him, Nay, my brother, do not force me ; for no such thing ought to be done in Israel : do not thou this folly. And I, whither shall I cause my shame to go? and as for thee, thou shalt be as one of the fools in Israel. Now, therefore, I pray thee, speak unto the king; for he will not withhold me from thee Howbeit he would not hearken unto her voice: but, being stronger than she, forced her, and lay with her.

Then Amnon hated her exceedingly: so that the hatred wherewith he hated her *is* greater than the love wherewith he had loved her. And Amnon said unto her, Arise, be gone. And she said unto him, *There* is no cause: this evil in sending me away is greater than the other that thou didst unto me. But he would not hearken unto her. Then he called his servant that ministered unto him, and said, Put now this *woman* out from me, and bolt the door after her. And she had a garment of divers colours upon her: for with such robes were the king's daughters *that were* virgins apparelled. Then his servant brought her out, and bolted the door after her.—2 Samuel XIII, 1-18.

Then said Absalom to Ahithophel, Give counsel among you what we shall do. And Ahithophel said unto Absalom, Go in unto thy father's concubines, which he hath left to keep the house; and all Israel shall hear that thou art abhorred of thy father: then shall the hands of all that *are* with thee be strong. So they spread Absalom a tent upon the top of the house; and Absalom went in unto his father's concubines in the sight of all Israel. And the counsel of Ahithophel, which he counselled in those days, was as if a man had enquired at the oracle of God: so *was* all the counsel of Ahithophel both with David and with Absalom.—2 Samuel XVI, 20-23.

Now king David was old *and* stricken in years: and they covered him with clothes, but he gat no heat Wherefore his servants said unto him, Let there be sought for my lord the king a young virgin: and let her stand before the king, and let her cherish him, and let her lie in thy bosom, that my lord the king may get heat. So they sought for a fair damsel throughout all the coasts of Israel, and found Abishag a Shunammite, and brought her to the king. And the damsel *was* very fair, and cherished the king, and ministered to him : but the king knew her not.—1 Kings I, 1-4.

Therefore, behold, I will bring evil upon the house of Jeroboam, and will cut off from Jeroboam him that pisseth against the wall, *and* him that is shut up and left in Israel, and will take away the remnant of the house of Jeroboam, as a man taketh away dung, till it be all gone.—1 Kings XIV, 10.

For the whole house of Ahab shall perish : and I will cut off from Ahab him that pisseth against the wall.—2 Kings IX, 8.

But Rab-shakeh said unto them, Hath my master sent me to thy master, and to thee, to speak these words ? *hath he* not *sent me* to the men which sit on the wall, that they may eat their own dung and drink their own piss with you.—2 Kings XVIII, 27.

Then said the king's servants that ministered unto him, Let there be fair young virgins sought for the king: And let the king appoint officers in all the provinces of his kingdom, that they may gather together all the fair young virgins unto Shushan the palace, to the house of the women, unto the custody of H-ge the king's chamberlain, keeper of the women : and let their things for purification be given *them :* And let the maiden which pleaseth the king be queen instead of Vashti. And the thing pleased the king ; and he did so.

Now when every maid's turn was come to go in to king Ahasuerus, after that she had been twelve months, according to the manner of the women. (for so were the days of their purification accomplished, *to wit*, six months with oil of myrrh, and six months with sweet odours, and with *other* things for the purifying of the women;) Then thus came *every* maiden unto the king ; whatsoever she desired was given her to go with her out of the house of the women unto the king's house. In the evening she went, and on the morrow she returned into the second house of the women, to the custody of

BIBLICAL ANTHOLOGY. 35

Shaashgaz, the king's chamberlain, which kept the concubines : she came in unto the king no more, except the king delighted in her, and that she were called by name.

Now when the turn of Esther, the daughter of Abihail the uncle of Mordecai, who had taken her for his daughter, was come to go unto the king, she required nothing but what Hegai the king's chamberlain, the keeper of the women, appointed. And Esther obtained favour in the sight of all them that looked upon her. So Esther was taken unto king Ahasuerus into his house royal in the tenth month, which *is* the month Tebeth, in the seventh year of his reign. And the king loved Esther above all the women, and she obtained g.ace and favour in his sight more than all the virgins ; so that he set the royal crown upon her head, and made her queen instead of Vashti.— Esther II, 2-4, 12-17.

Then the king returned out of the palace garden into the palace of the banquet of wine ; and Haman was fallen upon the bed whereon Esther *was*. Then said the king, Will he force the queen also before me in the house ? As the word went out of the king's mouth, they covered Haman's face.—Esther VII, 8.

Why died I not from the womb ? *why* did I not give up the ghost when I came out of the belly ?—Job III, 11.

Lo, now, his strength *is* in *his* loins, and his force *is* in the navel of his belly. He moveth his tail like a cedar : the sinews of his stones are wrapped together.—Job XL, 16-17.

My wounds stink *and* are corrupt because of my foolishness. I am troubled ; I am bowed down greatly ; I go mourning all the day long. For my loins are filled with a loathsome *disease:* and *there is* no soundness in my flesh. I am feeble and sore broken : I have roared by reason of the disquietness of my heart. Lord, all my desire *is* before thee ; and my groaning is not hid from thee. My heart panteth, my strength faileth me : as for the light of mine eyes, it also is gone from me. My lovers and my friends stand aloof from my sore ; and my kinsmen stand afar off.—Psalms xxxviii, 5-11.

Let thy fountain be blessed : and rejoice with the wife of thy youth. *Let her be as* the loving hind and pleasant roe ; let her breasts satisfy thee at all times ; and be thou ravished always with her love. And why wilt thou, my son, be ravished with a strange woman, and embrace the bosom of a stranger ?—Proverbs v, 18-20.

To keep thee from the evil woman, from the flattery of the tongue of a strange woman. Lust not after her beauty in thine heart ; neither let her take thee with her eyelids. For by means of a whorish woman *a man is brought* to a piece of bread : and the adulteress will hunt for the precious life.—Proverbs vi, 24-26.

For at the window of my house I looked through my casement, And beheld among the simple ones, I discerned among the youths, a young man void of understanding, Passing through the street near her corner ; and he went the way to her house, In the twilight, in the evening, in the black and dark night : And, behold, there met him a woman *with* the attire of an harlot, and subtil of heart. (She is loud and stubborn ; her feet abide not in her house : Now *is she* without, now in the streets, and lieth in wait at every corner.) So she caught him, and kissed him, *and* with an impudent face said unto him, *I have* peace offerings with me ; this day have I payed my vows. Therefore came I forth to meet thee, diligently to seek thy face, and I have found thee. I have decked my bed with coverings of tapestry, with carved *works*, with fine linen of Egypt. I have perfumed my bed with myrrh, aloes, and cinnamon. Come, let us take our fill of love until the morning : let us solace ourselves with loves. For the good man *is* not at home, he is gone a long journey : He hath taken a bag of money with him, *and* will come home at the day appointed. With her much fair speech she caused him to yield, with the flattering of her lips she forced him. He goeth after her straightway, as an ox goeth to the slaughter, or as a fool to the correction of the stocks; Till a dart strike through his liver ; as a bird hasteth to the snare, and knoweth not that it is for his life.—Proverbs VII, 6-23.

As thou knowest not what is the way of the spirit, nor how the bones *do grow* in the womb of her that is with child : even so thou knowest not the works of God who maketh all.—Ecclesiastes XI, 5.

How beautiful are thy feet with shoes, O prince's daughter ! the joints of thy thighs *are* like jewels, the work of the hands of a cunning workman. Thy navel is *like* a round goblet, which wanteth not liquor : thy belly is *like* an heap of wheat set about with lilies. Thy two breasts *are* like two young roes *that are* twins. Thy neck is as a tower of ivory ; thine eyes *like* the fishpools in Heshbon, by the gate of Bath-rabbim : thy nose is as the tower of Lebanon which looketh toward Damascus. Thine head upon thee *is* like Carmel, and the hair of thine head like purple ; the king *is* held in the galleries. How fair and how pleasant art thou, O love, for delights ! This thy stature is like to a palm tree, and thy breasts to clusters *of grapes*. I said I will go up to the palm tree, I will take hold of the boughs thereof : now also thy breasts shall be as clusters of the vine, and the smell of thy nose like apples ; And the roof of thy mouth like the best wine for my beloved, that goeth *down* sweetly, causing the lips of those that are asleep to speak.

I am my beloved's, and his desire *is* toward me. Come, my beloved, let us go forth into the field ; let us lodge in the villages. Let us get up early to the vineyards: let us see if the vine flourish, *whether* the tender grape appear, *and* the promegranates bud forth : there will I give thee my loves.—Solomon's Song VII, 1-12.

Therefore the LORD will smite with a scab the crown of the head of the daughters of Zion, and the LORD will discover their secret parts.—Isaiah III, 17.

Wherefore my bowels shall sound like an harp for Moab, and mine inward parts for Kir-haresh.—Isaiah XVI, 11.

So shall the king of Assyria lead away the Egyptians prisoners, and the Ethiopians captives, young and old, naked and barefoot, even with their buttocks uncovered, to the shame of Egypt.—Isaiah XX, 4.

Like as a woman with child, *that* draweth near the time of her delivery, is in pain, *and* crieth out in her pangs ; so have we been in thy sight, O LORD. We have been with child, we have been in pain, we have as it were brought forth wind ; we have not wrought any deliverance in the earth ; neither have the inhabitants of the world fallen.—Isaiah XXVI, 17-18.

Tremble, ye women that are at ease ; be troubled, ye careless ones : strip you, and make you bare, and gird *sackcloth* upon *your* loins. They shall lament for the teats, for the pleasant fields, for the fruitful vine.—Isaiah XXXII, 11-12.

But Rabshakeh said, Hath my master sent me to thy master and to thee to speak these words ? *hath he* not *sent me* to the men that sit upon the wall, that they may eat their own dung, and drink their own piss with you ?—Isaiah, XXXVI, 12.

Come down, and sit in the dust, O virgin daughter of Babylon, sit on the ground : *there is* no throne, O daughter of the Chaldeans : for thou shalt no more be called tender and delicate. Take the millstones, and grind meal : uncover thy locks, make bare the leg, uncover the thigh, pass over the rivers. Thy nakedness shall be uncovered, yea, thy shame shall be seen : I will take vengeance, and I will not meet *thee as* as a man.—Isaiah, XLVII, 1-3.

Behind the doors also and the posts hast thou set up thy remembrance : for thou hast discovered *thyself to another* than me, and art gone up; thou hast enlarged thy bed, and made thee *a covenant* with them; thou loved*st their bed where thou sawest *it*. And thou wentest to the king with ointment, and didst increase thy perfumes, and didst send thy messengers far off, and didst debase *thyself even* unto hell.—Isaiah LVII, 8-9.

Before she travailed, she brought forth; before her pain came, she was delivered of a man child. Who hath heard such a thing? who hath seen such things? Shall the earth be made to bring forth in one day? *or* shall a nation be born at once? for as soon as Zion travailed, she brought forth her children. Shall I bring to the birth, and not cause to bring forth? said the LORD: shall I cause to bring forth, and shut *the womb?* saith thy God. Rejoice ye with Jerusalem, and be glad with her, all ye that love her: rejoice for joy with her, all ye that mourn for her: That ye may suck. and be satisfied with the breasts of her consolations; that ye may milk out, and be delighted with the abundance of her glory.—Isaiah LXVI, 7-11.

Before I formed thee in the belly I knew thee; and before thou camest forth out of the womb I sanctified thee, *and* I ordained thee a prophet unto the nations.—Jeremiah I, 5.

For of old time I have broken thy yoke, *and* burst thy bands; and thou saidst, I will not transgress; when upon every high hill and under every green tree thou wanderest, playing the harlot.—Jeremiah II, 20.

They say, If a man put away his wife, and she go from him, and become another man's, shall he return unto her again? shall not that land be greatly polluted? but thou hast played the harlot with many lovers; yet return again to me, saith the LORD. Lift up thine eyes unto the high places, and see where thou hast not been lien with. In the ways hast thou sat for them, as the Arabian in the wilderness; and thou hast polluted the land with thy whoredoms and with thy wickedness. Therefore the showers have been withholden, and there hath been no latter rain; and thou hadst a whore's forehead, thou refusedst to be ashamed. Wilt thou not from this time cry unto me, My father, thou *art* the guide of my youth? Will he reserve *his anger* for ever? will he keep *it* to the end? Behold, thou hast spoken and done evil things as thou couldest.

The LORD said also unto me in the day of Josiah the king. Hast thou seen *that* which backsliding Israel hath done? she is gone up upon every high mountain and under every green tree, and there hath played the harlot. And I said after she had done all these *things*.Turn thou unto me. But she returned not And her treacherous sister Judah saw *it*. And I saw, wh n for all the causes whereby blacksliding Israel committed adultery I had put her away, and given her a bill of divorce; yet her treacherous sister Judah feared not, but went and played the harlot also. And it came to pass through the lightness of her whoredom, that she defiled the land, and committed adultery with stones and with stocks.—Jeremiah III, 1-9.

How shall I pardon thee for this? thy children have forsaken me, and sworn by *them that are* no gods: when I had fed them to the full, they then committed adultery, and assembled themselves by troops in the harlots' houses. They were *as* fed horses in the morning: every one neighed after his neighbour's wife.—Jeremiah v, 7-8.

What hath my beloved to do in mine house, *seeing* she hath wrought lewdness with many, and the holy flesh is passed from thee?—Jeremiah XI, 15.

Therefore will I discover thy skirts upon thy face, that thy shame may appear. I have seen thine adulteries, and thy neighings. the lewdness of thy whoredom, *and* thine abominations on the hills in the fields. Woe unto thee, O Jerusalem! wilt thou not be made clean? when *shall it* once be ?—Jeremiah XIII, 26-27.

Because he slew me not from the womb; or that my mother might have been my grave, and her womb *to be* always great *with me*. Wherefore came I forth out of the womb to see labour and sorrow, that my days should be consumed with shame?—Jeremiah xx. 17-18.

And these *are* the words that the LORD spake concerning Israel and concerning Judah. For thus saith the LORD : We have heard a voice of trembling, of fear, and not of peace. Ask ye now, and see whether a man doth travail with child? wherefore do I see every man with his hands on his loins, as a woman in travail, and all faces are turned into paleness.—Jeremiah xxx, 4-6.

Jerusalem hath grievously sinned ; therefore she is removed : all that honoured her despise her, because they have seen her nakedness : yea, she sigheth, and turneth backward. Her filthiness *is* in her skirts ; she remembered not her last end ; therefore she came down wonderfully.

Zion spreadeth forth her hands, *and there is* none to comfort her : the LORD hath commanded concerning Jacob, *that* his adversaries *should be* round about him : Jerusalem is as a menstruous woman among them.—Lamentations I, 8-9, 17.

And thou shalt eat it *as* barley cakes, and thou shalt bake it with dung that cometh out of man, in their sight. And the LORD said, Even thus shall the children of Israel eat their defiled bread among the Gentiles, whither I will drive them. Then said I, Ah, Lord GOD! behold, my soul hath not been polluted : for from my youth up even till now have I not eaten of that which dieth of itself, or is torn in pieces ; neither came their abominable flesh into my mouth. Then he said unto me, Lo, I have given thee cow's dung for man's dung, and thou shalt prepare thy bread therewith.—Ezekiel IV, 12-15.

And they that escape of you shall remember me among the nations, whither they shall be carried captives, because I am broken with their whorish heart, which hath departed from me, and with their eyes, which go a whoring after their idols: and they shall lothe themselves for the evils which they have committed in all their abominations.—Ezekiel VI, 9.

But thou didst trust in thine own beauty, and playedst the harlot because of thy renown, and pouredst out thy fornications on every one that passed by; his it was. And of thy garments thou didst take, and deckedst thy high places with divers colours, and playedst the harlot thereupon : *the like things* shall not come, neither shall it be *so*. Thou hast also taken thy fair jewels of my gold and of my silver, which I had given thee, and madest to thyself images of men, and didst commit whoredom with them.

Moreover thou hast taken thy sons and thy daughters, whom thou hast borne unto me, and these hast thou sacrificed unto them to be devoured. *Is this* of thy whoredoms a small matter?

And in all thine abominations and thy whoredoms thou hast not remembered the days of thy youth, when thou wast naked and bare, *and* was polluted in thy blood.

Thou hast built thy high place at every head of the way, and hast made thy beauty to be abhorred, and hast opened thy feet to every one that passed by, and multiplied thy whoredoms. Thou hast also committed fornication with the Egyptians thy neighbours, great of flesh ; and hast increased thy whoredoms, to provoke me to anger. Behold, therefore, I have stretched out my hand over thee, and have diminished thine ordinary *food*, and delivered thee unto the will of them that hate thee, the daughters of the Philistines, which are ashamed of thy lewd way. Thou hast played the whore also with the Assyrians, because thou wast unsatiable ; yea, thou hast played the harlot with them, and yet couldest not be satisfied. Thou hast moreover multiplied thy fornication in the land of Canaan unto Chaldea ; and yet thou wast not satisfied herewith. How weak is thine heart saith the Lord GOD, seeing thou doest all these *things*, the work of an imperious whorish woman ; In that thou buildest thine eminent place in the head of every way, and makest thine high place in every street ; and hast not been as an harlot, in that thou scornest hire ; *But as* a wife that committeth adultery, *which* taketh strangers instead of her husband ! They give gifts to all whores : but thou givest thy gifts to all thy lovers, and hirest them, that they may come unto thee on every side for thy whoredom. And the contrary is in thee from *other* women in thy whoredoms, whereas none followeth thee to commit whoredoms : and in that thou givest a reward, and no reward is given unto thee, therefore thou art contrary.

Wherefore, O harlot, hear the word of the LORD : Thus saith the Lord GOD ; Because thy filthiness was poured out, and thy nakedness discovered through thy whoredoms with thy lovers, and with all the idols of thy abominations, and by the blood of thy children, which thou didst give unto them ; Behold, therefore, I will gather all thy lovers, with whom thou hast taken pleasure, and all *them* that thou hast loved, with all *them* that thou hast hated ; I will even gather them round about against thee, and will discover thy nakedness unto them, that they may see all thy nakedness.—Ezekiel xvi, 15-17, 20, 22, 25-37.

And hath not eaten upon the mountains, neither hath lifted up his eyes to the idols of the house of Israel, neither hath defiled his neighbour's wife, neither hath come near to a menstruous woman.

And that doeth not any of those *duties*, but even hath eaten upon the mountains, and defiled his neighbour's wife.

That hath not eaten upon the mountains, neither hath lifted up his eyes to the idols of the house of Israel, hath not defiled his neighbour's wife.—Ezekiel xviii, 6, 11, 15.

In thee are men that carry tales to shed blood : and in thee they eat upon the mountains : in the midst of thee they commit lewdness. In thee have they discovered their fathers' nakedness : in thee have they humbled her that was set apart for pollution. And one hath committed abomination with his neighbour's wife ; and another hath lewdly defiled his daughter in law : and another in thee hath humbled his sister, his father's daughter.—Ezekiel xxii, 9-11.

44 BIBLICAL ANTHOLOGY.

The word of the LORD came again unto me, saying, Son of man, there were two women, the daughters of one mother : And they committed whoredoms in Egypt ; they committed whoredoms in their youth : there were their breasts pressed, and there they bruised the teats of their virginity. And the names of them *were* Aholah the elder, and Aholibah her sister : And they were mine, and they bare sons and daughters. Thus *were* their names ; Samaria *is* Aholah, and Jerusalem Aholibah. And Aholah played the harlot when she was mine ; and she doted on her lovers, on the Assyrians *her* neighbours, *Which were* clothed with blue, captains and rulers, all of them desirable young men, horsemen riding upon horses. Thus she committed her whoredoms with them, with all them *that were* the chosen men of Assyria, and with all on whom she doted ; with all their idols she defiled herself. Neither left she her whoredoms *brought* from Egypt : for in her youth they lay with her, and they bruised the breasts of her virginity, and poured their whoredom upon her. Wherefore I have delivered her into the hand of her lovers, into the hand of the Assyrians upon whom she doted. These discovered her nakedness : they took her sons and her daughters, and slew her with the sword : and she became famous among women ; for they had executed judgment upon her. And when her sister Aholibah saw *this*, she was more corrupt in her inordinate love than she, and in her whoredoms more than her sister in *her* whoredoms. She doted upon the Assyrians *her* neighbours, captains and rulers clothed most gorgeously, horsemen riding upon horses, all of them desirable young men. Then I saw that she was defiled, *that* they *took* both one way, And *that* she increased her whoredoms : for when she saw men pourtrayed upon the wall, the images of the Chaldeans pourtrayed with vermilion, Girded with girdles upon their loins, exceeding in dyed attire upon their heads, all of them princes to look to, after the manner of the Babylonians of Chaldea, the land of their nativity : And as soon as she saw them with her eyes, she doted upon them, and sent messengers unto them into Chaldea. And the Babylonians came to her into the bed of love, and they defiled her with their whoredom, and she was polluted with them, and her mind was alienated from them.

So she discovered her whoredoms, and discovered her nakedness: then my mind was alienated from her, like as my mind was alienated from her sister. Yet she multiplied her whoredoms, in calling to rememberance the days of her youth, wherein she had played the harlot in the land of Egypt. For she doted upon their paramours, whose flesh *is as* the flesh of asses, and whose issue *is like* the issue of horses. Thus thou calledst to rememberance the lewdness of thy youth, in bruising thy teats by the Egyptians for the paps of thy youth.

Therefore, O Aholibah, thus saith the Lord GOD; Behold, I will raise up thy lovers against thee, from whom thy mind is alienated, and I will bring them against thee on every side; The Babylonians and all the Chaldeans, Pekod, and Shoa, and Koa, *and* all the Assyrians with them: all of them desirable young men, captains and rulers, great lords and renowned, all of them riding upon horses. And they shall come against thee with chariots, wagons, and wheels, and with an assembly of people, *which* shall set against thee buckler and shield and helmet round about: and I will set judgment before them, and they shall judge thee according to their judgments. And I will set my jealously against thee, and they shall deal furiously with thee: they shall take away thy nose and thine ears; and thy remnant shall fall by the sword: they shall take thy sons and thy daughters; and thy residue shall be devoured by the fire. They shall also strip thee out of thy clothes, and take away thy fair jewels. Thus will I make thy lewdness to cease from thee, and thy whoredom *brought* from the land of Egypt: so that thou shalt not lift up thine eyes unto them, nor remember Egypt any more. For thus saith the Lord GOD; Behold, I will deliver thee into the hand *of them* whom thou hatest, into the hand *of them* from whom thy mind is alienated: And they shall deal with the hatefully, and shall take away all thy labour, and shall leave thee naked and bare: and the nakedness of thy whoredoms shall be discovered, both thy lewdness and thy whoredoms. I will do these *things* unto thee, because thou hast gone a whoring after the heathen, *and* because thou art polluted with their idols. Thou hast walked in the way of thy sister; therefore will I give her cup into thine hand. Thus saith the Lord GOD; Thou shalt drink of thy sister's cup deep and large: thou shalt be laughed to scorn and had in derision; it containeth much. Thou shalt be filled with drunkenness and sorrow, and the cup of astonishment and desolation, with the cup of thy sister Samaria. Thou shalt even drink it and suck *it* out, and thou shalt break the sherds thereof, and pluck off thine own breasts: for I have spoken *it*, saith the Lord GOD. Therefore thus saith the Lord GOD; Because thou hast forgotten me, and cast me behind thy back, therefore bear thou also thy lewdness and thy whoredoms.

The LORD said moreover unto me; Son of man, wilt thou judge Aholah and Aholibah? yea, declare unto them their abominations; That they have committed adultery, and blood *is* in their hands, and with their idols have they committed adultery, and have also caused their sons, whom they bare unto me, to pass for them through *the fire*, to devour *them*. Moreover this they have done unto me: they have defiled my sanctuary in the same day, and have profaned my sabbaths. For when they had slain their children to their idols, then they came the same day into my sanctuary to profane it; and, lo, thus have they done in the midst of mine house. And furthermore, that ye have sent for men to come from far, unto whom a messenger *was* sent; and, lo, they came: for whom thou didst wash thyself, paintedst thy eyes, and deckedst thyself with ornaments. And satest upon a stately bed, and a table prepared before it, whereupon thou hast set mine incense and mine oil. And a voice of a multitude being at ease *was* with her: and with the men of the common sort *were* brought Sabeans from the wilderness, which put bracelets upon their hands, and beautiful crowns upon their heads. Then said I unto *her that was* old in adulteries, Will they now commit whoredoms with her, and she *with them?* Yet they went in unto her, as they go in unto a woman that playeth the harlot: so went they in unto Aholah and unto Aholibah, the lewd women.

And the righteous men, they shall judge them after the manner of adulteresses, and after the manner of women that shed blood; because they *are* adulteresses, and blood *is* in their hands. For thus saith the

Lord GOD; I will bring up a company upon them, and will give them to be removed and spoiled. And the company shall stone them with stones, and dispatch them with their swords; they shall slay their sons and their daughters, and burn up their houses with fire. Thus will I cause lewdness to cease out of the land, that all women may be taught not to do after your lewdness. And they shall recompense your lewdness upon you, and ye shall bear the sins of your idols: and ye shall know that I *am* the Lord GOD.—Ezekiel XXIII, 1-49.

The beginning of the word of the LORD by Hosea. And the LORD said to Hosea, Go, take unto thee a wife of whoredoms and children of whoredoms: for the land hath committed great whoredom, *departing* from the LORD. So he went and took Gomer the daughter of Diblaim; which conceived and bare him a son.—Hosea I, 2-3.

Say ye unto your brethren, Ammi; and to your sisters, Ruhamah. Plead with your mother, plead: for she *is* not my wife, neither *am* I her husband; let her therefore put away her whoredoms out of her sight, and her adulteries from between her breasts; Lest I strip her naked, and set her as in the day that she was born, and make her as a wilderness, and set her like a dry land, and slay her with thirst. And I will not have mercy upon her children; for they *be* the children of whoredoms. For their mother hath played the harlot: she that conceived them hath done shamefully: for she said, I will go after my lovers, that give *me* my bread and my water, my wool and my flax, mine oil and my drink.

Therefore, behold, I will hedge up thy way with thorns, and make a wall, that she shall not find her paths. And she shall follow after her lovers, but she shall not overtake them; and she shall seek them, but shall not find *them:* then shall she say, I will go and return to my first husband; for then *was it* better with me than now. For she did not know that I gave her corn, and wine, and oil, and multiplied her silver and gold, *which* they prepared for Baal. Therefore will I return, and take away my corn in the time thereof, and my wine in the season thereof, and will recover my wool and my flax *given* to cover her nakedness. And now will I discover her lewdness in the sight of her lovers, and none shall deliver her out of mine hand. I will also cause all her mirth to cease, her feast days, her new moons, and her sabbaths, and all her solemn feasts. And I will destroy her vines and her fig trees, whereof she hath said, These *are* my rewards that my lovers have given me : and I will make them a forest, and the beasts of the field shall eat them. And I will visit upon her the days of Baalim, wherein she burned incense to them, and she decked herself with her earrings and her jewels, and she went after her lovers, and forgat me, saith the LORD.—Hosea II, 1-13.

Then said the LORD unto me, Go, yet, love a woman beloved of *her* friend, yet an adulteress, according to the love of the LORD toward the children of Israel, who look to other gods, and love flagons of wine. So I bought her to me for fifteen *pieces* of silver, and *for* an homer of barley, and an half homer of barley : And I said unto her, Thou shalt abide for me many days ; thou shalt not play the harlot, and thou shalt not be for *another* man : so *will* I also *be* for thee.—Hosea III, 1-3.

For they shall eat, and not have enough : they shall commit whoredom, and shall not increase : because they have left off to take heed to the LORD. Whoredom and wine and new wine take away the heart.

My people ask counsel at their stocks, and their staff declareth unto them : for the spirit of whoredoms hath caused them to err, and they have gone a whoring from under their God. They sacrifice upon the tops of the mountains, and burn incense upon the hills, under oaks and poplars and elms, because the shadow thereof *is* good ; therefore your daughters shall commit whoredom, and your spouses shall commit adultery. I will not punish your daughters when they commit whoredom, nor your spouses when they commit adultery : for themselves are separated with whores, and they sacrifice with harlots : therefore the people *that* doth not understand shall fall.

Though thou, Israel, play the harlot, *yet* let not Judah offend; and come not ye unto Gilgal, neither go ye up to Beth-aven, nor swear, The LORD liveth. For Israel slideth back as a backsliding heifer; now the LORD will feed them as a lamb in a large place. Ephraim *is* joined to idols : let him alone. Their drink is sour : they have committed whoredom continually : her rulers *with* shame do love, Give ye. The wind hath bound her up in her wings, and they shall be ashamed because of their sacrifices.—Hosea IV, 10-19.

I know Ephraim, and Israel is not hid from me : for now, O Ephraim, thou committest whoredom, *and* Israel is defiled. They will not frame their doings to turn unto their God : for the spirit of whoredoms *is* in the midst of them, and they have not known the LORD. Hosea V, 3-4.

And they have cast lots for my people ; and have given a boy for an harlot, and sold a girl for wine, that they might drink.—Joel III, 3.

And all the graven images thereof shall be beaten to pieces, and all the hires thereof shall be burned with the fire, and all the idols thereof will I lay desolate : for she gathered *it* of the hire of an harlot, and they shall return to the hire of an harlot. Therefore I will wail and howl, I will go stripped and naked : I will make a wailing like the dragons, and mourning as the owls.—Micah I, 7-8.

Because of the multitude of the whoredoms of the wellfavoured harlot, the mistress of witchcrafts, that selleth nations through her whoredoms, and families through her witchcrafts. Behold, I *am* against thee, saith the LORD of hosts : and I will discover thy skirts upon thy face, and I will shew the nations thy nakedness, and the kingdoms thy shame. And I will cast abominable filth upon thee, and make thee vile, and will set thee as a gazingstock.—Nahum III, 4.6.

Woe unto him that giveth his neighbour drink, that puttest thy bottle to *him*, and makest *him* drunken also, that thou mayest look on their nakedness ! Thou art filled with shame for glory : drink thou also, and let thy foreskin be uncovered : the cup of the LORD'S right hand shall be turned unto thee, and shameful spewing *shall be* on thy glory.—Habakkuk II, 15-16.

And I will bring distress upon men, that they shall walk like blind men, because they have sinned against the LORD ; and their blood shall be poured out as dust, and their flesh as the dung.—Zephaniah I, 17.

Behold I will corrupt your seed and spread dung upon your faces, even the dung of your solemn feasts.—Malachi II, 3.

Now the birth of Jesus Christ was on this wise : When as his mother Mary was espoused to Joseph, before they came together, she was found with child of the Holy Ghost. Then Joseph her husband, being a just *man*, and not willing to make her a public example, was minded to put her away privily. But while he thought on these things, behold, the angel of the LORD appeared unto him in a dream, saying. Joseph, thou son of David, fear not to take unto thee Mary thy wife : for that which is conceived in her is of the Holy Ghost.— Matthew I, 18-20.

For this cause God gave them up unto vile affections : for even their women did change the natural use into that which is against nature : And likewise also the men, leaving the natural use of the woman, burned in their lust one toward another ; men with men working that which is unseemly, and receiving in themselves that recompence of their error which was meet.—Romans I, 26-27.

It is reported commonly *that there is* fornication among you, and such fornication as is not so much as named among the Gentiles, that one should have his father's wife.—1 Corinthians v. 1.

Know ye not that the unrighteous shall not inherit the kingdom of God? Be not deceived : neither fornicators, nor idolaters, nor adulterers, nor effeminate, nor abusers of themselves with mankind, Nor thieves, nor covetous, nor drunkards, nor revilers, nor extortioners, shall inherit the kingdom of God. And such were some of you : but ye are washed, but ye are sanctified, but ye are justified in the name of the Lord Jesus, and by the Spirit of our God. All things are lawful unto me, but all things are not expedient : all things are lawful for me, but I will not be brought under the power of any. Meats for the belly, and the belly for meats : but God shall destroy both it and them. Now the body *is* not for fornication, but for the Lord ; and the Lord for the body. And God hath both raised up the Lord, and will also raise up us by his own power. Know ye not that your bodies are the members of Christ? shall I then take the members of Christ, and make *them* the members of an harlot? God forbid. What? know ye not that he which is joined to an harlot is one body? for two, saith he, shall be one flesh. But he that is joined unto the Lord is one spirit. Flee fornication. Every sin that a man doeth is without the body ; but he that committeth fornication sinneth against his own body.—1 Corinthians VI, 9-18.

Notwithstanding I have a few things against thee, because thou sufferest that woman Jezebel, which calleth herself a prophetess, to teach and to seduce my servants to commit fornication, and to eat things sacrificed unto idols. And I gave her space to repent of her fornication ; and she repented not. Behold, I will cast her into a bed, and them that commit adultery with her into great tribulation, except they repent of their deeds.—Revelations II, 20-22.

And there came one of the seven angels which had the seven vials, and talked with me, saying unto me, Come hither ; I will show unto thee the judgment of the great whore that sitteth upon many waters : With whom the kings of the earth have committeth fornication, and the inhabitants of the earth have been made drunk with the wine of her fornication. So he carried me away in the spirit into the wilderness : and I saw a woman sit upon a scarlet coloured beast, full of names of blasphemy, having seven heads and ten horns. And the woman was arrayed in purple and scarlet colour, and decked with gold and precious stones and pearls, having a golden cup in her hand full of abominations and filthiness of her fornication.—Revelations.— XVII, 1-4.

PART 2.
Passages illustrating the morality of the Bible.

Now the LORD had said unto Abram, Get thee out of thy country, and from thy kindred, and from thy father's house, unto a land that I will shew thee : And I will make of thee a great nation, and I will bless thee, and make thy name great ; and thou shalt be a blessing : And I will bless them that bless thee, and curse him that curseth thee : and in thee shall all families of the earth be blessed.

And Abram went down into Egypt to sojourn there, for the famine *was* grievous in the land. And it came to pass, when he was come near to enter into Egypt, that he said unto Sarai his wife, Behold now I know that thou *art* a fair woman to look upon : Therefore it shall come to pass, when the Egyptian shall see thee, that they shall say, This *is* his wife : and they will kill me, but they will save thee alive. Say, I pray thee, thou *art* my sister : * that it may be well with me for thy sake : and my soul shall live because of thee.—Genesis XII, 1-3, 10-13.

And when Abram was ninety years old and nine, the LORD appeared to Abram, and said unto him, I *am* the Almighty God ; walk before me, and be thou perfect.—Genesis XVII, 1.

And Abram journeyed from thence toward the south country, and dwelled between Kadesh and Shur, and sojourned in Gerar.

And Abram said of Sarah his wife, She *is* my sister : * and Abimelech king of Gerar sent, and took Sarah. But God came to Abimelech in a dream by night, and said to him, Behold thou *art but* a dead man, for the woman which thou hast taken ; for she *is* a man's

---

* Lying lips *are* abomination to the LORD.—Proverbs XII, 22.

wife. But Abimelech had not come near her : and he said, LORD, wilt thou slay also a righteous nation? Said he not unto me, She *is* my sister ? and she, even she herself said, He *is* my brother : in the integrity of my heart and innocency of my hands have I done this.—Genesis XX, 1-5.

And Sarah saw the son of Hagar the Egyptian, which she had borne unto Abraham, mocking. Wherefore she said unto Abraham, cast out this bondwoman, and her son : for the son of this bondwoman shall not be heir with my son, even with Isaac.

And Abraham rose up early in the morning and took bread and a bottle of water, and gave it unto Hagar, putting it on her shoulder, and the child, and sent her away : and she departed and wandered in the wilderness of Beersheba.—Genesis XXI, 9-10, 14.

And Abraham lifted up his eyes, and looked, and behold behind *him* a ram caught in a thicket by his horns : and Abraham went and took the ram, and offered him up for a burnt offering in the stead of his son.—Genesis XXII, 13.

And Isaac went unto Abimelech king of the Philistines unto Gorar. And the LORD appeared unto him, and said, Go not down into Egypt ; dwell in the land which I shall tell thee of : Sojourn in this land, and I will be with thee, and will bless thee : for unto thee, and unto thy seed, I will give all these countries.

And the men of the place asked him of his wife ; and he said, She is my sister, * for he feared to say, She is my wife ; lest said he, the men of the place should kill me for Rebekah : because she was fair to look upon. And it came to pass when he had been there a long time, that Abimelech king of the Philistines looked out at a window, and saw, and, behold, Isaac was sporting with Rebekah his wife. And Abimelech called Isaac, and said, Behold of a surety she is thy wife ; and how sayest thou, She is my sister? And Isaac said unto him, Because I said, lest I die for her.—Genesis XXVI, 1-3, 7-9.

---

* Lying lips are abomination to the LORD.—Proverbs XII, 22.

And the LORD appeared unto him the same night, and said, I am the God of Abraham thy father: fear not, for I am with thee, and will bless thee, and multiply thy seed for my servant Abraham's sake. And he builded an altar there and called upon the name of the LORD.—Genesis xxvi, 24-25.

And Isaac loved Esau, because he did eat of *his* venison: but Rebekah loved Jacob.—Genesis xxv, 28.

And it came to pass, that when Isaac was old, and his eyes were dim, so that he could not see, he called Esau his eldest son, and said unto him, My son: and he said unto him, Behold, *here am* I. And he said, Behold now, I am old, I know not the day of my death: Now therefore take, I pray thee, thy weapons, thy quiver and thy bow, and go out to the field, and take me *some* venison; And make me savoury meat, such as I love, and bring *it* to me, that I may eat; that my soul may bless thee before I die. And Rebekah heard when Isaac spake to Esau his son. And Esau went to the field to hunt *for* venison, *and* to bring *it*.

And Rebekah spake unto Jacob her son, saying, Behold, I heard thy father speak unto Esau thy brother, saying, Bring me venison, and make me savoury meat, that I may eat, and bless thee before the LORD before my death. Now therefore my son, obey my voice according to that which I command thee. Go now to the flock, and fetch me from thence two good kids of the goats; and I will make them savoury meat for thy father, such as he loveth. And thou shalt bring *it* to thy father, that he may eat, and that he may bless thee before his death. And Jacob said to Rebekah his mother, Behold, Esau my brother *is* a hairy man, and I *am* a smooth man: My father peradventure will feel me, and I shall seem to him as a deceiver; and I shall bring a curse upon me, and not a blessing. And his mother said unto him, Upon me *be* thy curse, my son: only obey my voice, and go fetch me *them*. And he went, and fetched, and brought *them* to his mother: and his mother made savoury meat, such as his father loved. And Rebekah took goodly raiment of her eldest son Esau, which were with her in the house, and put them upon Jacob her younger son : And she put the skins of the kids of the goats upon his hands, and upon the smooth of his neck : And she gave the savoury meat and the bread, which she had prepared, into the hand of her son Jacob.

And he came unto his father, and said, My father: and he said, Here am I ; who art thou, my son ? And Jacob said unto his father, I am Esau thy firstborn ; * I have done according as thou badest me : arise, I pray thee, sit and eat of my venison, that thy soul may bless me. And Isaac said unto his son, How is it that thou hast found it so quickly, my son ? And he said, Because the LORD thy God brought it to me. * And Isaac said unto Jacob, Come near, I pray thee, that I may feel thee, my son, whether thou be my very son Esau or not. And Jacob went near unto Isaac his father : and he felt him, and said, The voice is Jacob's voice, but the hands are the hands of Esau. And he discerned him not, because his hands were hairy, as his brother Esau's hands : so he blessed him. And he said, Art thou my very son Esau ? And he said, I am. * And he said, Bring it near to me, And I will eat of my son's venison, that my soul may bless thee. And he brought it near to him, and he did eat : and he brought him wine, and he drank. And his father Isaac said unto him, Come near now, and kiss me, my son. And he came near, and kissed him : and he smelled the smell of his raiment, and blessed him, and said, See the smell of my son is as the smell of a field which the LORD hath blessed : Therefore God give thee of the dew of heaven, and the fatness of the earth, and plenty of corn and wine : Let people serve thee, and nations bow down to thee : be lord over thy brethren, and let thy mother's sons bow down to thee : cursed be every one that curseth thee, and blessed be he that blesseth thee.

And he [Esau] said, Is he not rightly named Jacob ? for he hath supplanted me these two times : he took away my birthright : and behold, now he hath taken away my blessing.—Genesis XXVII, 1-29, 36.

---

* Lying lips are abomination to the LORD.—Proverbs XII, 22.

BIBLICAL ANTHOLOGY. 57

And Jacob went out from Beer-sheba, and went toward Haran, And he lighted upon a certain place, and tarried there all night, because the sun was set ; and he took of the stones of that place, and put *them* for his pillows, and lay down in that place to sleep. And he dreamed, and behold a ladder set up on the earth, and the top of it reached to heaven : and behold the angels of God ascending and descending on it. And, behold, the LORD stood above it, and said, I *am* the LORD God of Abraham thy father, and the God of Isaac : the land whereon thou liest, to thee will I give it, and to thy seed ; And thy seed shall be as the dust of the earth, and thou shalt spread abroad to the west, and to the east, and to the north, and to the south : and in thee and in thy seed shall all the families of the earth be blessed. And, behold, I *am* with thee, and will keep thee in all *places* whither thou goest, and will bring thee again into this land : for I will not leave thee, until I have done *that* which I have spoken to thee of.

And Jacob awaked out of his sleep, and he said, Surely the LORD is in this place.—Genesis XXVIII, 10-16.

And Laban had two daughters : the name of the elder *was* Leah, and the name of the younger *was* Rachel. Leah *was* tender eyed ; but Rachel was beautiful and well-favoured. And Jacob loved Rachel ; and said, I will serve thee seven years for Rachel thy younger daughter. And Laban said, *It is* better that I give her to thee, than that I should give her to another man : abide with me. And Jacob served seven years for Rachel ; and they seemed unto him *but* a few days, for the love he had to her. And Laban gathered together all the men of the place, and made a feast. And it came to pass in the evening, that he took Leah his daughter, and brought her to him ; and he went in unto her. And Laban gave unto his daughter Leah Zilpah his maid *for* an handmaid. And it came to pass, that in the morning, behold, it *was* Leah : and he said to Laban, What *is* this thou hast done unto me ? did not I serve with thee for Rachel ? wherefore then has thou beguiled me ? And Laban said, It must not be so done in our country, to give the younger before the firstborn. Fulfil her week, and we will give thee this also for the service which thou shalt serve with me yet seven other years. And Jacob did so, and fulfilled her week : and he gave him Rachel his daughter to wife also. And Laban gave to Rachel his daughter Bilhah his handmaid to be her maid. And he went in also unto Rachel, and he loved also Rachel more than Leah, and served with him yet seven other years. And when the LORD saw that Leah *was* hated, he opened her womb : but Rachel *was* barren. And Leah conceived, and bare a son, and she called his name Reuben : for she said, Surely the LORD hath looked upon my affliction ; now therefore my husband will love me. And she conceived again, and bare a son ; and said, Because the LORD hath heard that I *was* hated, he hath therefore given me this *son* also ; and she called his name Simeon. And she conceived again, and bare a son ; and said, Now this time will my husband be joined unto me, because I have born him three sons : therefore was his name called Levi. And she conceived again, and bare a son : and she said, Now will I praise the LORD : therefore she called his name Judah ; and left bearing.—Genesis XXIX, 16-35.

And Jacob did separate the lambs, and set the faces of the flocks toward the ringstraked, and all the brown in the flock of Laban ; and he put his own flocks by themselves, and put them not unto Laban's cattle. And it came to pass, whensoever the stronger cattle did conceive, that Jacob laid the rods before the eyes of the cattle in the gutters, that they might conceive among the rods. But when the cattle were feeble, he put *them* not in : so the feebler were Laban's, and the stronger Jacob's. And the man increased exceedingly, and had much cattle, and maidservants, and menservants, and camels, and asses.

And he heard the words of Laban's sons, saying, Jacob hath taken away all that *was* our father's : and of *that* which *was* our father's hath he gotten all this glory. And Jacob beheld the countenance of Laban, and, behold, it *was* not toward him as before. And the LORD said unto Jacob, Return unto the land of thy fathers, and to thy kindred ; and I will be with thee.

And Laban went to shear his sheep : and Rachel had stolen the images that *were* her father's. And Jacob stole away unawares to Laban the Syrian, in that he told him not that he fled. So he fled with all that he had.—Genesis xxx, 40-43 ; xxxi, 1-3, 19-21.

And Jacob was left alone ; and there wrestled a man with him until the breaking of the day. And when he saw that he prevailed not against him, he touched the hollow of his thigh ; and the hollow of Jacob's thigh was out of joint, as he wrestled with him. And he said, Let me go, for the day breaketh. And he said, I will not let thee go, except thou bless me. And he said unto him, What *is* thy name ? And he said, Jacob. And he said, Thy name shall be called no more Jacob, but Israel : for as a prince hast thou power with God and with men, and hast prevailed. And Jacob asked *him*, and said, Tell *me*, I pray thee, thy name. And he said, Wherefore *is* it *that* thou dost ask after my name? And he blessed him there. And Jacob called the name of the place Peniel : for I have seen God face to face, and my life is preserved.—Genesis xxxII, 24-30.

And God appeared unto Jacob again, when he came out of Padan-aram, and blessed him. And God said unto him, Thy name *is* Jacob : thy name shall not be called any more Jacob, but Israel shall be thy name : and he called his name Israel. And God said unto him, I am God Almighty : be fruitful and multiply ; a nation and a company of nations shall be of thee, and kings shall come out of thy loins ; And the land which I gave Abraham and Isaac, to thee I will give it, and to thy seed after thee will I give the land. And God went up from him in the place where he talked with him, and Jacob set up a pillar in the place where he talked with him, *even* a pillar of stone, and poured oil thereon. And Jacob called the name of the place where God spake with him, Beth-el.—Genesis xxxv, 9-15.

And unto Hamor and unto Shechem his son hearkened all that went out of the gate of his city ; and every male was circumcised, all that went out of the gate of his city. And it came to pass on the third day, when they were sore, that two of the sons of Jacob, Simeon and Levi, Dinah's brethren, took each man his sword, and came upon the city boldly, and slew all the males. And they slew Hamor and Shechem his son with the edge of the sword, and took Dinah out of Shechem's house, and went out. The sons of Jacob came upon the slain, and spoiled the city, because they had defiled their sister. They took their sheep, and their oxen, and their asses, and that which *was* in the city, and that which *was* in the field. And all their wealth, and all their little ones, and their wives took they captive, and spoiled even all that *was* in the house.—Genesis XXXIV, 24-29.

And it came to pass in those days, when Moses was grown, that he went out unto his brethren, and looked on their burdens : and he spied an Egyptian smiting an Hebrew, one of his brethren. And he looked this way and that way, and when he saw that *there was* no man, he slew the Egyptian, and hid him in the sand.—Exodus II, 11-12.

And I will give this people favour in the sight of the Egyptians : and it shall come to pass, that, when ye go, ye shall not go empty : But every woman shall borrow of her neighbour, and of her that sojourneth in her house, jewels of silver, and jewels of gold, and raiment : and ye shall put *them* upon your sons, and upon your daughters ; and ye shall spoil the Egyptians.

And the LORD said unto Moses, Yet will I bring one plague *more* upon Pharaoh, and upon Egypt ; afterwards he will let you go hence : when he shall let *you* go, he shall surely thrust you out hence altogether. Speak now in the ears of the people, and let every man borrow of his neighbour, and every woman of her neighbour, jewels of silver, and jewels of gold. And the LORD gave the people favour in the sight of the Egyptians. Moreover the man Moses *was* very great in the land of Egypt, in the sight of Pharoah's servants, and in the sight of the people.

And the children of Israel did according to the word of Moses ; and they borrowed of the Egyptians jewels of silver, and jewels of gold, and raiment : And the LORD gave the people favour in the

BIBLICAL ANTHOLOGY. 61

sight of the Egyptians, so that they lent unto them *such things as they required.* And they spoiled the Egyptians.—Exodus III, 21-22 ; XI, 1-3 ; XII, 35-36.

And the LORD said unto Moses, When thou goest to return into Egypt, see that thou do all those wonders before Pharaoh, which I have put in thine hand : but I will harden his heart, that he shall not let the people go.—Exodus IV, 21.

And the LORD said unto Moses, See, I have made thee a god to Pharaoh : And Aaron thy brother shall be thy prophet.

And I will harden Pharaoh's heart, and multiply my signs and my wonders in the land of Egypt. But Pharaoh shall not hearken unto you, that I may lay my hand upon Egypt, and bring forth mine armies, *and* my people the children of Israel, out of the land of Egypt by great judgments.

And he hardened Pharaoh's heart, that he hearkened not unto them ; as the LORD had said. And the LORD said unto Moses, Pharaoh's heart *is* hardened, he refuseth to let the people go.—Exodus VII, 1, 3-4, 13-14.

The LORD *is* a man of war.—Exodus XV, 3.

I the LORD thy God *am* a jealous God, visiting the iniquity of the fathers upon the children unto the third and fourth *generation* of them that hate me. * —Exodus XX, 5.

And if a man smite his servant, or his maid, with a rod, and he die under his hand ; he shall be surely punished. Notwithstanding,

* The fathers shall not be put to death for the children, neither shall the children be put to death for the fathers : every man shall be put to death for his own sin.—Deuteronomy XXIV, 16.
But he slew not their children, but *did* as *it is* written in the law in the book of Moses, where the LORD commanded, saying, The fathers shall not die for the children, neither shall the children die for the fathers, but every man shall die for his own sin.—2 Chronicles XXV, 4.
The son shall not bear the iniquity of the father, neither shall the father bear the iniquity of the son.—Ezekiel XVIII, 20.

if he continue a day or two, he shall not be punished ; for he *is* his money.—Exodus XXI, 20-21.

Ye shall keep the sabbath therefore; for it *is* holy unto you : every one that defileth it shall surely be put to death : for whosoever doeth *any* work therein, that soul shall be cut off from among his people. Six days may work be done ; but in the seventh *is* the sabbath of rest, holy to the LORD : whosoever doeth *any* work in the sabbath day, he shall surely be put to death.

For in six days the LORD made heaven and earth, and on the seventh day he rested, and was refreshed.—Exodus XXXI, 14-15, 17.

And while the children of Israel were in the wilderness, they found a man that gathered sticks upon the sabbath day. And they that found him gathering sticks brought him unto Moses and Aaron, and unto all the congregation. And they put him in ward, because it was not declared what should be done to him. And the LORD said unto Moses, The man shall be surely put to death : all the congregation shall stone him with stones without the camp. And all the congregation brought him without the camp, and stoned him with stones, and he died ; as the LORD commanded Moses.—Numbers XV, 32-36.

Thou shalt not suffer a witch to live.—Exodus XXII, 18.

A man also, or woman that hath a familiar spirit, or that is a wizard, shall surely be put to death ; they shall stone them with stones : their blood shall be upon them.—Leviticus XX, 27.

And when Moses saw that the people were naked ; (for Aaron had made them naked unto *their* shame among their enemies :) Then Moses stood in the gate of the camp, and said, Who *is* on the LORD's side ? *let him come* unto me. And all the sons of Levi gathered themselves together unto him. And he said unto them, Thus saith the LORD God of Israel, Put every man his sword by his side, *and* go in and out from gate to gate throughout the camp, and slay every man his brother, and every man his companion, and every man his neighbour. And the children of Levi did according to the word of Moses: and there fell of the people that day about three thousand men. For Moses had said, Consecrate yourselves to day to the LORD, even every man upon his son, and upon his brother; that he may bestow upon you a blessing this day.—Exodus xxxii, 25-29.

And the Israelitish woman's son blasphemed the name *of the Lord*, and cursed. And they brought him unto Moses: And they put him in ward, that the mind of the LORD might be shewed them. And the LORD spake unto Moses, saying, Bring forth him that hath cursed without the camp: and let all that heard *him* lay their hands upon his head, and let all the congregation stone him. And thou shalt speak unto the children of Israel, saying, Whosoever curseth his God shall bear his sin. And he that blasphemeth the name of the the LORD, he shall surely be put to death, *and* all the congregation shall certainly stone him : as well the stranger, as he that is born in the land, when he blasphemeth the name *of the Lord*, shall be put to death.

And Moses spake to the children of Israel, that they should bring forth him that had cursed out of the camp, and stone him with stones. And the children of Israel did as the LORD commanded Moses.—Leviticus xxiv, 11-16, 23.

Both thy bondmen, and thy bondmaids, which thou shalt have, *shall* be of the heathen that are round about you; of them shall ye buy bondmen and bondmaids. Moreover of the children of the strangers that do sojourn among you, of them shall ye buy, and of their families that *are* with you, which they begat in your land : and they shall be your possession. And ye shall take them as an inheritance for your children after you, to inherit *them for* a possession; they shall be your bondmen forever : but over your brethren the children of Israel, ye shall not rule one over another with rigour.— Leviticus xxv, 44-46.

Notwithstanding no devoted thing, that a man shall devote unto the LORD of all that he hath, *both* of man and beast, and of the field of his possession, shall be sold or redeemed : every devoted thing *is* most holy unto the LORD. None devoted, which shall be devoted of men, shall be redeemed ; *but* shall surely be put to death.—Leviticus xxvii, 28-29.

And *when* the people complained, it displeased the LORD : and the LORD heard *it ;* and his anger was kindled ; and the fire of the LORD burnt among them, and consumed *them that were* in the uttermost parts of the camp.—Numbers xi, 1.

And the LORD said unto Moses, If her father had but spit in her face, should she not be ashamed seven days ? let her be shut out from the camp seven days.—Numbers xii, 14.

And Israel abode in Shittim, and the people began to commit whoredom with the daughters of Moab. And they called the people unto the sacrifices of their god : and the people did eat, and bowed down to their gods. And Israel joined himself unto Baal-peor : and the anger of the LORD was kindled against Israel. And the LORD said unto Moses, Take all the heads of the people, and hang them up before the LORD against the sun, that the fierce anger of the LORD may be turned away from Israel. And Moses said unto the judges of Israel, Slay ye every one his men that were joined unto Baal-peor. And, behold, one of the children of Israel came and brought unto his brethren a Midianitish woman in the sight of Moses, and in the sight of all the congregation of the children of Israel, who *were* weeping *before* the door of the tabernacle of the congregation. And when Phinehas, the son of Eleazar, the son of Aaron the priest, saw *it,* he rose up from among the congregation, and took a javelin in his hand ; And he went after the man of Israel into the tent, and thrust both of them through, the man of Israel, and the woman through her belly. So the plague was stayed from the children of Israel. And those that died in the plague were twenty and four thousand.—Numbers xxv, 1-9.

BIBLICAL ANTHOLOGY. 65

But Sihon king of Heshbon would not let us pass by him : for the LORD thy God hardened his spirit, and made his heart obstinate, that he might deliver him into thy hand, as *appeareth* this day. And the LORD said unto me, Behold, I have begun to give Sihon and his land before thee : begin to possess, that thou mayest inherit his land. Then Sihon came out against us, he and all his people, to fight at Jahaz. And the LORD our God delivered him before us ; and we smote him, and his sons, and all his people. And we took all his cities at that time, and utterly destroyed the men, and the women, and the little ones, of every city, we left none to remain : Only the cattle we took for a prey unto ourselves, and the spoil of the cities which we took.—Deuteronomy II, 30-35.

And the LORD said unto me, Fear him not : for I will deliver him, and all his people, and his land, into thy hand ; and thou shalt do unto him as thou didst unto Sihon king of the Amorites, which dwelt at Heshbon. So the LORD our God delivered into our hands Og also, the king of Bashan, and all his people : and we smote him until none was left to him remaining. And we took all his cities at that time, there was not a city which we took not from them, threescore cities, all the region of Argob, the kingdom of Og in Bashan. All these cities *were* fenced with high walls, gates, and bars ; beside unwalled towns a great many. And we utterly destroyed them, as we did unto Sihon king of Heshbon, utterly destroying the men, women, and children, of every city. But all the cattle, and the spoil of the cities, we took for a prey to ourselves.—Deuteronomy III, 2-7.

I the LORD thy God *am* a jealous God, visiting the iniquity of the fathers upon the children unto the third and fourth *generation* of of them that hate me. * —Deuteronomy v, 9.

---

* The fathers shall not be put to death for the children ; neither shall the children be put to death for the fathers : every man shall be put to death for his own sin.—Deuteronomy xxiv, 16.

But he slew not their children, but *did* as *it is* written in the law in the books of Moses, where the LORD had commanded, saying, The fathers shall not die for the children, neither shall the children die for the fathers, but every man shall die for his own sin.—2 Chronicles xxv, 4.

The son shall not bear the iniquity of the father, neither shall the father bear the iniquity of the son.—Ezekiel xviii, 20.

BIBLICAL ANTHOLOGY.

When the LORD thy God shall bring thee into the land whither thou goest to possess it, and hath cast out many nations before thee, the Hittites, and the Girgashites, and the Amorites, and the Canaanites, and the Perizzites, and the Hivites, and the Jebusites, seven nations greater and mightier than thou; And when the LORD thy God shall deliver them before thee; thou shalt smite them, *and* utterly destroy them ; thou shalt make no covenant with them, nor shew mercy unto them. Neither shalt thou make marriages with them ; thy daughter thou shalt not give unto his son, nor his daughter shalt thou take unto thy son. For they will turn away thy son from following me, that they may serve other gods : so will the anger of the LORD be kindled against you, and destroy thee suddenly. But thus shall ye deal with them; ye shall destroy their altars, and break down their images, and cut down their groves, and burn their graven images with fire. For thou *art* an holy people unto the LORD thy God : the LORD thy God hath chosen thee to be a special people unto himself, above all people that *are* upon the face of the earth. *

The LORD did not set his love upon you, nor choose you, because ye were more in number than any people ; for ye *were* the fewest of all people : But because the Lord loved you, and because he would keep the oath, which he had sworn unto your fathers, hath the LORD brought you out with a mighty hand, and redeemed you out of the house of bondmen, from the hand of Pharaoh king of Egypt. Know therefore that the LORD thy God, he *is* God, the faithful God, which keepeth covenant and mercy with them that love him and keep his commandments to a thousand generations ; And repayeth them that hate him to their face, to destroy them : he will not be slack to him that hateth him, he will repay him to his face.

Thou shalt be blessed above all people : there shall not be male or female barren among you, or among your cattle. And the LORD will

---

* *There is* no iniquity with the LORD our God, nor respect of persons.—2 Chronicles XIX, 7.
But glory, honour, and peace, to every man that worketh good, to the Jew first, and also to the Gentile : For there is no respect of persons with God.—Romans II, 10-14.
Your Master also is in heaven ; neither is there respect of persons with him.—Ephesians VI, 9.

take away from thee all sickness, and will put none of the evil diseases of Egypt, which thou knowest, upon thee ; but will lay them upon all *them* that hate thee. And thou shalt consume all the people which the LORD thy God shall deliver thee ; thine eye shall have no pity upon them.

Moreover the LORD thy God will send the hornet among them, until they that are left, and hide themselves from thee, be destroyed. Thou shalt not be affrighted at them : for the LORD thy God *is* among you, a mighty God and terrible. And the LORD thy God will put out those nations before thee by little and little ; thou mayest not consume them at once, lest the beasts of the field increase upon thee : But the LORD thy God shall deliver them unto thee, and shall destroy them with a mighty destruction, until they be destroyed. And he shall deliver their kings into thine hand, and thou shalt destroy their name from under heaven ; there shall no man be able to stand before thee, until thou have destroyed them.—Deuteronomy VII, 1-10, 14-16, 20-24.

Take heed to yourselves, that your heart be not deceived, and ye turn aside, and serve other gods and worship them ; And *then* the LORD's wrath be kindled against you, and he shut up the heaven, that there be no rain, and that the land yield not her fruit; and *lest* ye perish quickly from off the good land which the LORD giveth you.—Deuteronomy XI, 16-17.

If thy brother, the son of thy mother, or thy son, or thy daughter, or the wife of thy bosom, or thy friend, which *is* as thine own soul, entice thee secretly, saying, Let us go and serve other gods, which thou hast not known, thou, nor thy fathers ; *Namely*, of the gods of the people which *are* round about you, nigh unto thee, or far off from thee, from the *one* end of the earth even unto the *other* end of the earth ; Thou shalt not consent unto him, nor hearken unto him ; neither shall thine eye pity him, neither shalt thou spare, neither shalt thou conceal him : But thou shalt surely kill him ; thine hand shall be first upon him to put him to death, and afterwards the hand of all the people,

And thou shalt stone him with stones that he die.—Deuteronomy XIII, 6-10.

If thou shalt hear *say* in one of thy cities, which the LORD thy God hath given thee to dwell there, saying, *Certain* men, the children of Belial, are gone out from among you, and have withdrawn the inhabitants of their city, saying, Let us go and serve other gods, which ye have not known; Then shalt thou enquire, and make search, and ask diligently; and, behold, *if it be* truth, *and* the thing certain, *that* such abomination is wrought among you; Thou shalt surely smite the inhabitants of that city with the edge of the sword, destroying it utterly, and all that *is* therein, and the cattle thereof, with the edge of the sword. And thou shalt gather all the spoil of it into the midst of the street thereof, and shalt burn with fire the city, and all the spoil thereof every whit, for the LORD thy God: and it shall be an heap for ever; it shall not be built again. And there shall cleave nought of the cursed thing to thine hand: that the LORD may turn from the fierceness of his anger, and shew thee mercy, and have compassion upon thee, and multiply thee, as he hath sworn unto thy fathers.—Deuteronomy XIII, 12-17

Ye shall not eat *of* any thing that dieth of itself: thou shalt give it unto the stranger that *is* in thy gates, that he may eat it; or thou mayest sell it unto an alien: for thou *art* an holy people unto the LORD thy God.—Deuteronomy XIV, 21.

And thou shalt bestow that money for whatsoever thy soul lusteth after, for oxen, or for sheep, or for wine, or for strong drink, or for whatsoever thy soul desireth.—Deuteronomy XIV, 26.

When thou comest nigh unto a city to fight against it, then proclaim peace unto it. And it shall be, if it make thee answer of peace, and open unto thee, then it shall be, *that* all the people *that is* found therein shall be tributaries unto thee, and they shall serve thee. And if it will make no peace with thee, but will make war against thee, then thou shalt besiege it : And when the LORD thy God hath delivered it into thine hands, thou shalt smite every male thereof with the edge of the sword : But the women, and the little ones, and the cattle, and all that is in the city, *even* all the spoil thereof, shalt thou take unto thyself ; and thou shalt eat the spoil of thine enemies, which the LORD thy God hath given thee. Thus shalt thou do unto all the cities *which are* very far off from thee, which *are* not of the cities of these nations. But of the cities of these people, which the LORD thy God doth give thee *for* an inheritance, thou shalt save alive nothing that breatheth : But thou shalt utterly destroy them ; *namely*, The Hittites, and the Amorites, the Canaanites, and the Perizzites, the Hivites, and the Jebusites ; as the LORD thy God hath commanded thee.—Deuteronomy xx, 10-17.

If a man have a stubborn and rebellious son, which will not obey the voice of his father, or the voice of his mother, and *that*, when they have chastened him, will not hearken unto them : Then shall his father and his mother lay hold on him, and bring him out unto the elders of his city, and unto the gate of his place ; And they shall say unto the elders of his city, This our son *is* stubborn and rebellious, he will not obey our voice ; *he is* a glutton, and a drunkard. And all the men of his city shall stone him with stones, that he die.—Deuteronomy XXI, 18-21.

And Joshua the son of Nun was full of the spirit of wisdom ; for Moses had laid his hands upon him ; and the children of Israel hearkened unto him.— Deuteronomy XXXIV, 9.

Now after the death of Moses the servant of the LORD it came to pass, that the LORD spake unto Joshua the son of Nun, Moses' minister, saying, Moses my servant is dead ; now therefore arise, go over this Jordan, thou, and all this people, unto the land which I do give to them, *even* to the children of Israel. Every place that the sole of your foot shall tread upon, that have I given unto you, as I said unto Moses. From the wilderness and this Lebanon even unto the great river, the river Euphrates, all the land of the Hittites, and unto the great sea toward the going down of the sun, shall be your coast. There shall not any man be able to stand before thee all the days of thy life ; as I was with Moses, *so* I will be with thee : I will not fail thee, nor forsake thee. Be strong and of a good courage ; for unto this people shalt thou divide for an inheritance the land, which I sware unto their fathers to give them. Only be thou strong and very courageous, that thou mayest observe to do according to all the law, which Moses my servant commanded thee: turn not from it *to* the right hand or *to* the left, that thou mayest prosper whithersoever thou goest. This book of the law shall not depart out of thy mouth; but thou shalt meditate therein day and night, that thou mayest observe to do according to all that is written therein ; for then thou shalt make thy way prosperous, and then thou shalt have good success. Have not I commanded thee? Be strong and of a good courage ; be not afraid, neither be thou dismayed; for the LORD thy God *is* with thee whithersoever thou goest.—Joshua I, 1-9,

On that day the LORD magnified Joshua in the sight of all Israel ; and they feared him, as they feared Moses, all the days of his life.— Joshua IV, 14.

And they utterly destroyed all that *was* in the city [Jericho], both man and woman, young and old, and ox, and sheep, and ass, with the edge of the sword.—Joshua VI, 21.

So the LORD was with Joshua ; and his fame was *noised* throughout all the country.—Joshua VI, 27.

And the LORD said unto Joshua, Fear not, neither be thou dismayed : take all the people of war with thee, and arise, go up to Ai : see, I have given into thy hand the king of Ai, and his people, and his city, and his land : And thou shalt do to Ai and her king as thou didst unto Jericho and her king : only the spoil thereof, and the cattle thereof, shall ye take for a prey unto yourselves : lay thee an ambush for the city behind it. And the LORD said unto Joshua, Stretch out the spear that *is* in thy hand toward Ai; for I will give it into thine hand. And Joshua stretched out the spear that *he had* in his hand toward the city. And the ambush arose quickly out of their place, and they ran as soon as he had stretched out his hand ; and they entered the city, and took it, and hasted and set the city on fire. And when the men of Ai looked behind them, they saw, and, behold, the smoke of the city ascended up to heaven, and they had no power to flee this way or that way ; and the people that fled to the wilderness turned back upon the pursuers. And when Joshua and all Israel saw that the ambush had taken the city, and that the smoke of the city ascended, then they turned again, and slew the men of Ai. And the other issued out of the city against them ; so they were in the midst of Israel, some on this side, and some on that side ; and they smote them, so that they let none of them remain or escape. And the king of Ai they took alive, and brought him to Joshua. And it came to pass, when Israel had made an end of slaying all the inhabitants of Ai in the field, in the wilderness wherein they chased them, and when they were all fallen on the edge of the sword, until they were consumed, that all the Israelites returned unto Ai, and smote it with the edge of the sword. And *so* it was, *that* all that fell that day, both of men and women, *were* twelve thousand, *even* all the men of Ai. For Joshua drew not his hand back, wherewith he stretched out the spear, until he had utterly destroyed all the inhabitants of Ai. Only the cattle and the spoil of that city Israel took for a prey unto themselves, according unto the word of the LORD which he commanded Joshua. And Joshua burnt Ai, and made it an heap for ever, *even* a desolation unto this day. And the king of Ai he hanged on a tree until eventide : and as soon as the sun was down, Joshua commanded that they should take his carcase down from the tree, and cast it at the entering of the gate of the city, and raise thereon a great heap of stones, *that remaineth* unto this day.

Then Joshua built an altar unto the LORD God of Israel in mount Ebal.—Joshua VIII, 1-2, 18-30.

And it came to pass, as they fled from before Israel, and were in the going down to Beth-horon, that the LORD cast down great stones from heaven upon them unto Azekah, and they died ; *they were more which died with hailstones than they whom the children of Israel slew with the sword.*—Joshua x, 11.

But these five kings fled, and hid themselves in a cave at Makkedah. And it was told Joshua, saying, The five kings are found hid in a cave at Makkedah. And Joshua said, Roll great stones upon the mouth of the cave, and set men by it for to keep them : And stay ye not, *but* pursue after your enemies, and smite the hindmost of them ; suffer them not to enter into their cities : for the LORD your God hath delivered them into your hand.

And it came to pass, when Joshua and the children of Israel had made an end of slaying them with a very great slaughter till they were consumed, that the rest *which* remained of them entered into fenced cities. And all the people returned to the camp to Joshua at Makkedah in peace : none moved his tongue against any of the children of Israel. Then said Joshua, Open the mouth of the cave, and bring out those five kings unto me out of the cave. And they did so, and brought forth those five kings unto him out of the cave, the king of Jerusalem, the king of Hebron, the king of Jarmuth, the king of Lachish, *and* the king of Eglon. And it came to pass when they brought out those kings unto Joshua, that Joshua called for all the men of Israel, and said unto the captains of the men of war which went with him. Come near, put your feet upon the necks of these kings. And they came near, and put their feet upon the necks of them. And Joshua said unto them, Fear not, nor be dismayed, be strong and of good courage : for thus shall the LORD do to all your enemies against whom ye fight. And afterwards Joshua smote them, and slew them, and hanged them on five trees : and they were hanging upon the trees until the evening.—Joshua x, 16-26.

And the LORD said unto Joshua, Be not afraid because of them : for to-morrow about this time will I deliver them up all slain before Israel : thou shalt hough * their horses, and burn their chariots with

---

* " HOUGH, to disable by cutting the sinews of the ham."—Stormonth's English Dictionary.

fire. So Joshua came, and all the people of war with him, against them by the waters of Merom suddenly; and they fell upon them. And the LORD delivered them into the hand of Israel, who smote them, and chased them unto great Zidon, and unto Misrephcth-miam, and unto the valley of Mizpeh eastward ; and they smote them, until they left them none remaining. And Joshua did unto them as the LORD bade him : he houghed their horses, and burnt their chariots with fire.—Joshua XI, 6-9.

And Joshua at that time turned back, and took Hazor, and smote the king thereof with the sword : for Hazor beforetime was the head of all those kingdoms. And they smote all the souls that *were* therein with the edge of the sword, utterly destroying *them* ; there was not any left to breathe : and he burnt Hazor with fire. And all the cities of those kings, and all the kings of them, did Joshua take, and smote them with the edge of the sword, *and* he utterly destroyed them, as Moses the servant of the LORD commanded. But *as for* the cities that stood still in their strength, Israel burned none of them, save Hazor only ; *that* did Joshua burn. And all the spoil of these cities, and the cattle, the children of Israel took for a prey unto themselves : but every man they smote with the edge of the sword, until they had destroyed them, neither left they any to breathe.

As the LORD commanded Moses his servant, so did Moses command Joshua, and so did Joshua ; he left nothing undone of all that the LORD commanded Moses. So Joshua took all that land, the hills, and all the south country, and all the land of Goshen, and the valley, and the plain, and the mountain of Israel, and the valley of the same ; *Even* from the mount Halak, that goeth up to Seir, even unto Baal-gad in the valley of Lebanon under mount Hermon; and all their kings he took, and smote them, and slew them. Joshua made war a long time with all those kings. There was not a city that made peace with the children of Israel, save the Hivites the inhabitants of Gibeon: all *other* they took in battle. For it was of the LORD to harden their hearts, that they should come against Israel in battle, that he might destroy them utterly, *and* that they might have no favour, but that he might destroy them, as the LORD commanded Moses.

And at that time came Joshua, and cut off the Anakims from the mountains, from Hebron, from Debir, from Anab, and from all the mountains of Judah, and from all the mountains of Israel : Joshua destroyed them utterly with their cities.—Joshua xi, 10-21.

Now Joshua was old *and* stricken in years : and the LORD said unto him, Thou art old *and* stricken in years, and there remaineth yet very much land to be possessed.—Joshua xiii, 1.

Therefore we will also serve the LORD: for he *is* our God. And Joshua said unto the people, Ye cannot serve the LORD: for he *is* an holy God; he is a jealous God; he will not forgive your transgressions nor your sins. If ye forsake the LORD, and serve strange gods, then he will turn and do you hurt, and consume you.—Joshua xxiv, 18-20.

Howbeit Sisera fled away on his feet to the tent of Jael the wife of Heber the Kenite : for *there* was peace between Jabin the king of Hazor and the house of Heber the Kenite.

And Jael went out to meet Sisera, and said unto him, Turn in, my lord, turn in to me; fear not. And when he had turned in unto her into the tent, she covered him with a mantle. And he said unto her, Give me, I pray thee, a little water to drink ; for I am thirsty. And she opened a bottle of milk, and gave him drink, and covered him. Again he said unto her, Stand in the door of the tent, and it shall be, when any man doth come and enquire of thee, and say, Is there any man here? thou shalt say, No. And Jael Heber's wife took a nail of the tent, and took an hammer in her hand, and went softly unto him, and smote the nail into his temples, and fastened it into the ground : for he was fast asleep and weary. So he died. And, behold, as Barak pursued Sisera, Jael came out to meet him, and said unto him, Come, and I will show thee the man whom thou seekest. And when he came into her *tent*, behold, Sisera lay dead, and the nail *was* in his temples.

Blessed above women shall Jael the wife of Heber the Kenite be, blessed shall she be above women in the tent. He asked water, *and* she gave *him* milk ; she brought forth butter in a lordly dish. She put her hand to the nail, and her right hand to the workman's hammer ; and with the hammer she smote Sisera, she smote off his head, when she had pierced and stricken through his temples. At her feet he bowed, he fell, he lay down : at her feet he bowed, he fell: where he bowed, there he fell down dead. The mother of Sisera looked out at a window, and cried through the lattice, Why is his chariot *so* long in coming.? why tarry the wheels of his chariots ?— Judges IV, 17-22 ; v, 24-28.

Notwithstanding no devoted thing, that a man shall devote unto the LORD of all that he hath, *both* of man and beast, and of the field of his possession, shall be sold or redeemed : every devoted thing *is* most holy unto the LORD. None devoted, which shall be devoted of men, shall be redeemed; *but* shall surely be put to death.—Leviticus XXVII, 28-29.

Then the Spirit of the LORD came upon Jephthah, and he passed over Gilead, and Manasseh, and passed over Mizpeh of Gilead, and from Mizpeh of Gilead he passed over *unto* the children of Ammon.

And Jephthah vowed a vow unto the LORD, and said, If thou shalt without fail deliver the children of Ammon into my hands, Then it shall be, that whatsoever cometh forth of the doors of my house to meet me, when I return in peace from the children of Ammon, shall surely be the LORD's, and I will offer it up for a burnt offering.

So Jephthah passed over unto the children of Ammon to fight against them ; and the LORD delivered them into his hands. * And he smote them from Aroer, even till thou come to Minnith, *even* twenty cities, and unto the plain of the vineyards, with a very great slaughter. Thus the children of Ammon were subdued before the children of Israel. *

And Jephthah came to Mizpeh unto his house, and, behold, his daughter came out to meet him with timbrels and with dances : and

---

* "That the LORD spake unto me saying, Thou art to pass over through Ar, the coast of Moab this day: And when thou comest nigh over against the children of Ammon, distress them not, nor meddle with them ; for I will not give thee of the land of the children of Ammon *any* possession ; because I have given it unto the children of Lot *for* a possession."—Deuteronomy II, 17-19.

she *was his* only child'; and beside her he had neither son nor daughter. And it came to pass, when he saw her, that he rent his clothes, and said, Alas, my daughter! thou has brought me very low, and thou art one of them that trouble me : for I have opened my mouth unto the LORD and I cannot go back. And she said unto him, My father, *if* thou hast opened thy mouth unto the LORD, do to me according to that which hath proceeded out of thy mouth ; forasmuch as the LORD hath taken vengance for thee of thine enemies, *even* of the children of Ammon. And she said unto her father, Let this thing be done for me : let me alone two months, that I may go up and down upon the mountains, and bewail my virginity, I and my fellows. And he said, Go. And he sent her away *for* two months; and she went with her companions, and bewailed her virginity upon the mountains. And it came to pass at the end of two months, that she returned unto her father, who did with her *according* to his vow which he had vowed; and she knew no man.—Judges XI, 29-39.

And he smote the men of Beth-Shemesh, because they had looked into the ark of the LORD, even he smote of the people fifty thousand and three score and ten men : and the people lamented, because the LORD had smitten many of the people with a great slaughter.—1 Samuel VI, 19.

Now there was a man of Benjamin, whose name *was* Kish. And he had a son, whose name *was* Saul, a choice young man, and a goodly : and *there was* not among the children of Israel a goodlier person than he : from his shoulders and upward *he was* higher than any of the people.

Now the LORD had told Samuel in his ear a day before Saul came, saying, To-morrow about this time I will send thee a man out of the land of Benjamin, and thou shalt anoint him *to be* captain over my people Israel, that he may save my people out of the hand of the Philistines : for I have looked upon my people, because their cry is come unto me. And when Samuel saw Saul, the LORD said unto him, Behold the man whom I spake to thee of ! this same shall reign over my people.

Then Samuel took a vial of oil, and poured *it* upon his head, and kissed him, and said, *Is it* not because the LORD hath anointed thee *to be* captain over his inheritance ?—Samuel IX, 1-2, 15-17 ; X, 1.

Samuel also said unto Saul, The LORD sent me to anoint thee to *be* king over his people, over Israel: now therefore hearken thou unto the voice of the words of the LORD. Thus saith the LORD of hosts, I remember that which Amalek did to Israel, how he laid wait for him in the way when he came up from Egypt. Now go, and smite Amalek, and utterly destroy all that they have, and spare them not; but slay both man and woman, infant and suckling, ox and sheep, camel and ass.

And Saul smote the Amalekites from Havilah *until* thou comest to Shur, that *is* over against Egypt. And he took Agag the king of the Amalekites alive, and utterly destroyed all the people with the edge of the sword. But Saul and the people spared Agag, and the best of the sheep, and of the oxen, and of the fatlings, and the lambs, and all *that was* good, and would not utterly destroy them : but every thing *that was* vile and refuse, that they destroyed utterly.

Then came the word of the LORD unto Samuel, saying, It repenteth me that I have set up Saul *to be* king : for he is turned back from following me, and hath not performed my commandments. And it grieved Samuel ; and he cried unto the LORD all night. And when Samuel rose early to meet Saul in the morning, it was told Samuel, saying, Saul came to Carmel, and behold, he set him up a place, and is gone about, and passed on, and gone down to Gilgal. And Samuel came to Saul : And Saul said unto him, Blessed *be* thou of the LORD : I have performed the commandment of the LORD. And Samuel said, What *meaneth* then this bleating of the sheep in mine ears, and the lowing of the oxen which I hear ? And Saul said, They have brought them from the Amalekites : for the people spared the best of the sheep and of the oxen, to sacrifice unto the LORD thy God ; and the rest we have utterly destroyed. Then Samuel said unto Saul, Stay, and I will tell thee what the LORD hath said to me this night. And he said unto him, Say on. And Samuel said, When thou *wast* little in thine own sight, *wast* thou not *made* the head of the tribes of Israel, and the LORD anointed thee king over Israel? And the LORD sent thee on a journey, and said, Go and utterly destroy the sinners the Amalekites, and fight against them until they be consumed. Wherefore then didst thou not obey the voice of the LORD, but didst fly upon the spoil, and didst evil in the sight of the LORD? And Saul said unto Samuel, Yea, I have obeyed the voice of the LORD, and have gone the way which the LORD sent me, and have brought Agag the king of Amalek, and have utterly destroyed the Amalekites. But the people took of the spoil, sheep and oxen, the chief of the things which should have been utterly destroyed, to sacrifice unto the LORD thy God in Gilgal. And Samuel said, Hath the LORD *as great* delight in burnt offerings and sacrifices, as in obeying the voice of the LORD? Behold, to obey *is* better than sacrifice, and to hearken than the fat of rams. For rebellion *is as* the sin of witchcraft, and stubbornness *is as* iniquity and idolatry. Because thou hast rejected the word of the LORD, he hath also rejected thee from *being* king.

And Saul said unto Samuel, I have sinned: for I have transgressed the commandment of the LORD, and thy words; because I feared the people, and obeyed their voice. Now therefore, I pray thee, pardon my sin, and turn again with me, that I may worship the LORD. And Samuel said unto Saul, I will not return with thee: for thou hast rejected the word of the LORD, and the LORD hath rejected thee from being king over Israel.

Then said Samuel, Bring ye hither to me Agag the king of the Amalekites. And Agag came unto him delicately. And Agag said, Surely the bitterness of death is past. And Samuel said, As thy sword hath made women childless, so shall thy mother be childless among women. And Samuel hewed Agag in pieces before the LORD in Gilgal.—1 Samuel xv, 1-3, 7-26, 32-33.

And the LORD said unto Samuel, How long wilt thou mourn for Saul, seeing I have rejected him from reigning over Israel? fill thine horn with oil, and go, I will send thee to Jesse the Bethlehemite: for I have provided me a king among his sons. And

Samuel said, How can I go ? if Saul hear it, he will kill me. And the LORD said, Take an heifer with thee, and say, I am come to sacrifice to the LORD. *—1 Samuel XVI, 1-2.

But the Spirit of the LORD departed from Saul, and an evil spirit from the LORD troubled him. And Saul's servants said unto him, Behold now, an evil spirit from God troubleth thee.—1 Samuel XVI. 14-15.

And David arose, and fled that day for fear of Saul, and went to Achish the King of Gath. And the servants of Achish said unto him, Is not this David the king of the land? did they not sing one to another of him in dances, saying, Saul hath slain his thousands, and David his ten thousands ? And David laid up these words in his heart, and was sore afraid of Achish the king of Gath. And he changed his behaviour before them, and feigned himself mad in their hands, and scrabbled on the doors of the gate, and let his spittle fall down upon his beard.—1 Samuel XXI, 10-13.

And David gathered all the people together, and went to Rabbah, and fought against it, and took it. And he took their king's crown from off his head, the weight whereof was a talent of gold, with the precious stones, and it was set on David's head. And he brought forth the spoil of the city in great abundance. And he brought forth the people that were therein, and put them under saws and under harrows of iron, and under axes of iron, and made them pass through the brick-kiln : and thus did he unto all the cities of the children of Ammon.—2 Samuel XII, 29-31.

And they set the ark of God upon a new cart, and brought it out of the house of Abinadab that was in Gibeah : and Uzzah and Ahio, the sons of Abinadab, drave the new cart.

And when they came to Nachon's threshingfloor, Uzzah put forth his hand to the ark of God, and took hold of it, for the oxen shook

---
* "1 Samuel sent by God, under pretence of a sacrifice, cometh to Beth-lehem."— Head-note to chapter XVI.

it. And the anger of the LORD was kindled against Uzzah; and God smote him there for *his* error ; and there he died by the ark of God. And David was displeased because the LORD had made a breach upon Uzzah : and he called the name of the place Perez-uzzah to this day·
—2 Samuel VI, 3, 6-8.

Then there was a famine in the days of David three years, year after year ; and David enquired of the LORD, And the LORD answered, *It is* for Saul, and for *his* bloody house because he slew the Gibeonites.
—2 Samuel XXI, 1.

And again the anger of the LORD was kindled against Israel, and he moved David against them to say, Go, number Israel and Judah. And Joab and the captains of the host went out from the presence of the king, to number the people of Israel..

And Joab gave up the sum of the number of the people unto the king ; and there were in Israel eight hundred thousand valiant men that drew the sword ; and the men of Judah *were* five hundred thousand men.

And David's heart smote him after that he had numbered the people. And David said unto the LORD, I have sinned greatly in that I have done : and now, I beseech thee, O LORD, take away the iniquity of thy servant ; for I have done very foolishly. For when David was up in the morning the word of the LORD came unto the prophet Gad, David's seer, saying, Go and say unto David, thus saith the LORD, I offer thee three *things*; choose thee one of them that I may *do it* unto thee. So Gad came to David, and told him, and said unto him, Shall seven years of famine come upon thee in thy land ? or wilt thou flee three months before thine enemies, while they pursue thee ? or that there be three days' pestilence in thy land ? now advise, and see what answer I shall return to him that sent me. And David said unto Gad, I am in a great strait : let us fall now into the hand of the LORD ; for his mercies *are* great: and let me not fall into the hand of man.

So the LORD sent a pestilence upon Israel from the morning even to the time appointed ; and there died of the people from Dan even

BIBLICAL ANTHOLOGY. 31

to Beer-sheba seventy thousand men. And when the angel stretched out his hand upon Jerusalem to destroy it, the LORD repented him of the evil, and said to the angel that destroyed the people, It is enough: stay now thine hand. And the angel of the LORD was by the threshingplace of Araunah the Jebusite. And David spake unto the LORD when he saw the angel that smote the people, and said, Lo, I have sinned, and I have done wickedly : but these sheep, what have they done?—2 Samuel XXIV 1, 4, 9-17.

And Satan stood up against Israel, and provoked David to number Israel. And David said to Joab and to the rulers of the people, Go, number Israel from Beer-sheba even to Dan : and bring the number of them to me, that I may know *it*. And Joab answered, The LORD make his people an hundred times so many more as they *be :* but, my lord the king, *are* they not all my lord's servants? why then doth my lord require this thing? why will he be a cause of trespass to Israel ? Nevertheless the king's word prevailed against Joab. Wherefore Joab departed, and went throughout all Israel, and came to Jerusalem.

And Joab gave the sum of the number of the people unto David. And all *they of* Israel were a thousand thousand and an hundred thousand men that drew sword : and Judah *was* four hundred threescore and ten thousand men that drew sword. But Levi and Benjamin counted he not among them : for the king's word was abominable to Joab. And God was displeased with this thing; therefore he smote Israel. And David said unto God, I have sinned greatly, because I have done this thing; but now, I beseech thee, do away the iniquity of thy servant ; for I have done very foolishly.

And the LORD spake unto Gad, David's seer, saying, Go and tell David, saying, Thus saith the LORD, I offer thee three *things* : choose thee one of them, that I may do *it* unto thee. So Gad came to David, and said unto him, Thus saith the LORD, choose thee Either three years' famine : or three months to be destroyed before thy foes, while that the sword of thine enemies overtaketh *thee* : or else three days the sword of the LORD, even the pestilence, in the land,

BIBLICAL ANTHOLOGY.

and the angel of the LORD destroying throughout all the coasts of Israel. Now therefore advise thyself what word I shall bring again to him that sent me. And David said unto Gad, I am in a great strait : Let me fall now into the hand of the LORD ; for very great *are* his mercies : But let me not fall into the hand of man.

So the LORD sent pestilence upon Israel, and there fell of Israel seventy thousand men. And God sent an angel unto Jerusalem to destroy it : and as he was destroying, the LORD beheld, and he repented him of the evil, and said to the angel that destroyed, It is enough, stay now thine hand. And the angel of the LORD stood by the threshingfloor of Ornan the Jebusite. And David lifted up his eyes, and saw the angel of the LORD stand between the earth and the heaven. having a drawn sword in his hand stretched out over Jerusalem. Then David and the elders *of Israel, who were* clothed in sackcloth, fell upon their faces. And David said unto God, *Is it* not I *that* commanded the people to be numbered ? even I it is that have sinned and done evil indeed ; but *as for* these sheep, what have they done ? let thine hand, I pray thee, O LORD my God, be on me, and on my father's house ; but not on thy people that they should be plagued.—1 Chronicles XXI, 1-17.

Now the days of David drew nigh that he should die ; and he charged Solomon his son, saying,

Behold, *thou hast* with thee Shimei the son of Gera, a Benjamite of Bahurim, which cursed me with a grievous curse in the day when I went to Mahanaim : but he came down to meet me at Jordan, and I sware to him by the LORD saying. I will not put thee to death with the sword. Now therefore hold him not guiltless ; for thou *art* a wise man, and knowest what thou oughtest to do unto him ; but his hoar head bring thou down to the grave with blood. So David slept with his fathers, and was buried in the city of David.—1 Kings II, 1, 8-10.

Go, tell Jeroboam, Thus saith the LORD God of Israel,

Thou hast not been as my servant David, who kept my commandments, and who followed me with all his heart, to do *that* only *which was* right in mine eyes.—1 Kings XIV, 7, 8.

I have found David the *son* of Jesse, a man after mine own heart, which shall fulfil all my will.—Acts XIII, 22.

And God gave Solomon wisdom and understanding exceeding much, and largeness of heart, even as the sand that *is* on the sea shore. And Solomon's wisdom excelled the wisdom of all the children of the east country, and all the wisdom of Egypt. For he was wiser than all men.—1 Kings IV, 29-31.

But king Solomon loved many strange women, together with the daughter of Pharaoh, women of the Moabites, Ammonites, Edomites, Zidonians, *and* Hittites ; Of the nations *concerning* which the LORD said unto the children of Israel, Ye shall not go in to them, neither shall they come in unto you : *for* surely they will turn away your heart after their gods : Solomon clave unto these in love. And he had seven hundred wives, princesses, and three hundred concubines : and his wives turned away his heart.—1 Kings XI, 1-3.

And the LORD said, Who shall persuade Ahab, that he may go up and fall at Ramoth-gilead ? And one said on this manner, and another said on that manner. And there came forth a spirit, and stood before the LORD, and said, I will persuade him. And the LORD said unto him, Wherewith ? And he said, I will go forth, and I will be a lying spirit in the mouth of all his prophets. And he said, Thou shalt persuade *him*; and prevail also : go forth, and do so. Now therefore, behold, the LORD hath put a lying spirit in the mouth of all these thy prophets, and the LORD hath spoken evil concerning thee.—1 Kings XXII, 20-23.

And Elijah answered and said to the captain of fifty, if I be a man of God, then let fire come down from heaven, and consume thee and thy fifty, and there came down fire from heaven and consumed him and his fifty.—2 Kings I, 10.

And he went up from thence unto Bethel : and as he was going up by the way, there came forth little children out of the city, and mocked him, and said unto him. Go up, thou bald head ; go up, thou bald head. And he turned back, and looked on them, and cursed them in the name of the LORD. And there came forth two she bears out of the wood, and tare forty and two children of them.—2 Kings II, 23-24.

So Jehu slew all that remained in the house of Ahab in Jezreel, and all his great men, and his kinsfolks, and his priests, until he left him none remaining.

And the LORD said unto Jehu, Because thou hast done well in executing that which is right in mine eyes, and hast done unto the house of Ahab according to all that was in mine heart, thy children of the fourth generation shall sit on the throne of Israel.—2 Kings x, 11, 30.

And the LORD said, Who shall entice Ahab king of Israel, that he may go up and fall at Ramoth-gilead ? And one spake saying after this manner, and another saying after that manner. Then there came out a spirit and stood before the LORD, and said, I will entice him. And the LORD said unto him, Wherewith ? And he said, I will go out and be a lying spirit in the mouth of all his prophets. And the Lord said, Thou shalt entice him, and thou shalt also prevail ; go out, and do even so. Now, therefore, behold, the LORD hath put a lying spirit in the mouth of these thy prophets, and the LORD hath spoken evil concerning thee.—2 Chronicles XVIII, 19-22.

Set thou a wicked man over him ; and let Satan stand at his right hand. When he shall be judged, let him be condemned ; and let his prayer become sin. Let his days be few ; *and* let another take his office. Let his children be fatherless, and his wife a widow. Let his children be continually vagabonds, and beg ; let them seek *their bread* also out of their desolate places. Let the extortioner catch all that he hath ; and let the strangers spoil his labour. Let there be none to extend mercy unto him : neither let there be any to favour his fatherless children. Let his posterity be cut off ; *and* in the generation following let their name be blotted out. Let the iniquity of his fathers be remembered with the LORD ; and let not the sin of his mother be blotted out.—Psalms CIX, 6-14.

The LORD hath made all things for himself ; yea, even the wicked for the day of evil.—Proverbs XVI, 4.

O LORD, thou hast deceived me, and I was deceived: thou art stronger than I, and hast prevailed : I am in derision daily, every one mocketh me.—Jeremiah XX, 7.

Therefore thou shalt say unto them, Thus saith the LORD of Hosts, the God of Israel, Drink ye and be drunken, and spue, and fall, and rise no more, because of the sword which I will send among you.—Jeremiah XXV, 27.

And I will make drunk her princes, and her wise men, her captains, and her rulers, and her mighty men ; and they shall sleep a perpetual sleep, and not wake, saith the king, whose name is the LORD of Hosts.—Jeremiah LI, 57.

And if the prophet be deceived when he hath spoken a thing, I the LORD have deceived that prophet, and I will stretch out mine hand upon him, and will destroy him from the midst of my people Israel. —Ezekiel XIV, 9.

Wherefore I gave them also statutes *that were* not good, and judgments whereby they should not live.—Ezekiel XX, 25.

Beat your ploughshares into swords, and your pruning hooks into spears ; let the weak say, I am strong.—Joel III, 10.

But I say unto you, that ye resist not evil; but whosoever shall smite thee on thy right cheek, turn to him the other also.— Matthew V, 39.

And, whosoever shall not receive you, nor hear your words, when ye depart out of that house, or city, shake off the dust of your feet. Verily, I say unto you, it shall be more tolerable for the land of Sodom and Gomorrah, in the day of judgment, than for that city.— Matthew x, 14-15.

Think not that I am come to send peace on earth : I came not to send peace, but a sword. For I am come to set a man at variance against his father, and the daughter against her mother, and the daughter-in-law against her mother-in-law.*—Matthew x, 34-35.

But I say unto you, That every idle word that men shall speak, they shall give account thereof in the day of judgment.—Matthew xii, 36.

And he said unto them, unto you it is given to know the mystery of the kingdom of God, but unto them that are without, all *these* things are done in parables ; That seeing they may see, and not perceive, and hearing they may hear, and not understand ; lest at any time they should be converted, and *their* sins should be forgiven them.—Mark iv, 11-13.

Now there was there, nigh unto the mountain, a great herd of swine feeding. And all the devils besought him, saying, Send us into the swine, that we may enter into them. And forthwith Jesus gave them leave. And the unclean spirits went out, and entered into the swine : and the herd ran violently down a steep place into the sea (they were about two thousand) and were choked in the sea.— Mark v, 11-13.

And when they came nigh to Jerusalem, unto Bethphage, and Bethany, at the Mount of Olives, he sendeth forth two of his disciples, And saith unto them, go your way into the village over against you; and, as soon as ye be entered into it, ye shall find a colt tied, whereon

---

* "For God is not the *author of* confusion, but of peace."—1 Corinthians xiv, 33.

never man sat ; loose him, and bring *him*. And if any man say unto you, Why do ye this? Say ye that the LORD hath need of him ; and straightway he will send him hither.—Mark XI, 1-3.

And on the morrow, when they were come from Bethany, he was hungry. And seeing a fig-tree afar off, having leaves, he came, if haply he might find anything thereon ; and when he came to it, he found nothing but leaves ; for the time of figs was not *yet*. And Jesus answered and said unto it, No man eat fruit of thee hereafter for ever. And his disciples heard *it*.

And in the morning, as they passed by, they saw the fig-tree dried up from the roots. And Peter calling to remembrance, saith unto him, Master, behold the fig-tree which thou cursedst is withered away.—Mark XI, 12-14, 20-21.

He that believeth, and is baptized shall be saved ; but he that believeth not shall be damned.—Mark XVI, 16.

I am come to send fire on the earth ; and what will I, if it be already kindled? But I have a baptism to be baptized with ; and how am I straitened till it be accomplished ! Suppose ye that I am come to give peace on earth? I tell you, Nay ; but rather division : For from henceforth there shall be five in one house divided, three against two, and two against three. The father shall be divided against the son, and the son against the father ; the mother against the daughter, and the daughter against the mother ; the mother-in-law against her daughter-in-law, and the daughter-in-law against her mother-in-law.*
—Luke XII, 49-53.

If any *man* come to me, and hate not his father, and mother, and wife, and children, and brethren, and sisters, yea, and his own life also, he cannot be my disciple.—Luke XIV, 26.

And he said unto them that stood by, Take from him the pound, and give *it* to him that hath ten pounds. (And they said unto him,

---

* "For God is not *the author* of confusion, but of peace."—1 Corinthians XIV, 33.

LORD, he hath ten pounds.) For I say unto you, That unto every one which hath shall be given ; and from him that hath not, even that he hath shall be taken away from him. But those mine enemies, which would not that I should reign over them, bring hither, and slay *them* before me.—Luke XIX, 24-27.

Then said he unto them, But now he that hath a purse, let him take *it*, and likewise *his* scrip ; and he that hath no sword let him sell his garment and buy one.—Luke XXII, 36.

Then took they him [Christ] and led *him* and brought him into the high priest's house, and Peter followed afar off. And when they had kindled a fire in the midst of the hall, and were set down together, Peter sat down among them. But a certain maid beheld him, as he sat by the fire, and earnestly looked upon him, and said, This man was also with him. And he denied him, saying, Woman I know him not. And after a little while another saw him, and said, Thou art also of them. And Peter said, Man I am not.—Luke XXII, 54-58.

Then Simon Peter having a sword drew it, and smote the high priest's servant, and cut off his right ear. The servant's name was Malchus.—John XVIII, 10.

And it shall come to pass *that* every soul which will not hear that prophet shall be destroyed from among the people.—Acts III, 23.

But Elymas the sorcerer (for so is his name by interpretation) withstood them, seeking to turn away the deputy from the faith. Then Saul (who also *is called* Paul) filled with the Holy Ghost, set his eyes on him, and said, O full of all subtlety and all mischief, *thou* child of the devil, *thou* enemy of all righteousness, wilt thou not cease to pervert the right ways of the LORD. And now, behold the hand of the LORD *is* upon thee, and thou shalt be blind, not seeing the sun for a season. And immediately there fell on him a mist and a darkness; and he went about seeking some to lead him by the hand.—Acts XIII, 8-11.

And some days after, Paul said unto Barnabas, Let us go again and visit our brethren in every city where we have preached the word of the LORD, *and see* how they do. And Barnabas determined to take with them John, whose surname was Mark. But Paul thought not good to take him with them, who departed from them from Pamphylia, and went not with them to the work. And the contention was so sharp between them, that they departed asunder, one from the other; and so Barnabas took Mark, and sailed unto Cyprus. And Paul chose Silas, and departed, being recommended by the brethren unto the grace of God.—Acts XV, 36-40.

For if the truth of God hath more abounded through my lie unto his glory, why yet am I also judged as a sinner.—Romans III, 7.

Let every soul be subject unto the higher powers. For there is no power but of God: the powers that be are ordained of God. Whosoever therefore resisteth the power, resisteth the ordinance of God: and they that resist shall receive to themselves damnation.—Romans XIII, 1-2.

But if any man be ignorant, let him be ignorant.—1 Corinthians XIV, 38.

If any man love not the LORD Jesus Christ, let him be Anathema Maran-atha.—1 Corinthians XVI, 22.

I robbed other churches, taking wages *of them*, to do you service.—2 Corinthians XI, 8.

But be it so, I did not burden you, nevertheless, being crafty, I caught you with guile.—2 Corinthians XII, 16.

BIBLICAL ANTHOLOGY.

As we said before, so say I now again, if any *man* preach any other gospel unto you than that ye have received, let him be accursed.—Galatians I, 9.

I would they were even cut off which trouble you.—Galatians v, 12.

And for this cause God shall send them strong delusion, that they should believe a lie : That they all might be damned who believed not the truth, but had pleasure in unrighteousness.—2 Thessalonians II. 11-12.

A man that is an heretick after the first and second admonition reject.—Titus III, 10.

If there come any unto you, and bring not this doctrine, receive him not into *your* house, neither bid him God speed.—2 John, 10.

And there was war in heaven : Michael and his angels fought against the dragon ; and the dragon fought and his angels.—Revelations XII. 7.

And he *was* clothed with a vesture dipped in blood : and his name is called the Word of God. And the armies *which were* in heaven followed him upon white horses, clothed in fine linen, white and clean. And out of his mouth goeth a sharp sword, that with it he should smite the nations: and he shall rule them with a rod of iron : and he treadeth the winepress of the fierceness and wrath of Almighty God.—Revelations XIX, 13-15.

He that is unjust, let him be unjust still : and he which is filthy, let him be filthy still.—Revelations XXII, 11.

THE END.

BIBLICAL ANTHOLOGY:

A COLLECTION OF PASSAGES ILLUSTRATING THE PURITY AND
MORALITY OF THE HOLY BIBLE.

Crown 8vo, Limp Cloth, 75 cts, Paper Covers, 50 cts.

"Goethe, being once in Kiel, was invited to attend a meeting called by some clergymen, for the suppression of obscene literature. He attended, and proposed that they should begin with the Bible. That ended the conference, and it was never heard of again. And that will end all these attempts to suppress books called immoral by prurient imaginations, just so soon as the same measure is meted out to Freethinkers and Bible Societies."—See *Liberty and Morality*, a Lecture, by MONCURE D. CONWAY, pp. 10-11.

"It is surely time for the rulers of Christian Churches in general, and for those of the Established Church in particular, to consider whether the sacred books of the Hebrews ought any longer to be presented as they are now to Christian people as pictures of the Divine character and of the Divine dealings with mankind. Historical philosophy reads them with a discriminating eye. It severs the tribal and the primæval from the universal, that which is perennially moral, such as most of the Commandments in the Decalogue, from that which by the progress of humanity has ceased to be so. It marks, in the midst of that which is utterly unspiritual and belongs merely to primitive society or to the Semite of Palestine, the faint dawn of the spiritual, and traces its growing brightness down through the writings of prophets and psalmists till it becomes day. But the people are not historical philosophers. Either they will be misled by the uncritical reading of the Old Testament or they will be repelled. Hitherto they have been misled, and some of the darkest pages of Christian history, including that which records the maltreatment of the Jews, in so far as it was religious, have been the result of their aberrations. Now they are being repelled, and the repulsion is growing stronger and more visible every day. It is not necessary, and it may be irritating, to rehearse the long series of equivocal passages which shocked the moral sense of Bishop Colenso, and of which Mr. Ingersoll, the great apostle of Agnosticism in America, makes use in his popular lectures with terrible effect. The question is one of the most practical kind, and it will not well brook delay. It is incomparably more urgent than that of Biblical Revision."—GOLDWIN SMITH in the *Nineteenth Century* for October, 1881 ; reprinted in the *Canadian Monthly* for February, 1882, pp. 211-212.

For Sale at the principal Bookstores, or mailed, post-paid, on receipt of price, by

JONES & BELFORD,
PUBLISHERS,

TORONTO, ONT.

www.ingramcontent.com/pod-product-compliance
Lightning Source LLC
Chambersburg PA
CBHW020257090426
42735CB00009B/1120